THE MASTERPIECE
AND THE MAN

W. B. YEATS, *circa* 1936

The Masterpiece and the Man

YEATS AS I KNEW HIM

Monk Gibbon

The Macmillan Company
New York
1959

Printed in Great Britain by Butler & Tanner Ltd, Frome and London

TO

MICHAEL FRANKLIN

ILLUSTRATIONS

ACKNOWLEDGEMENTS

THE publisher and author wish to express their gratitude to the following people for permission to quote copyright material: to Mrs Yeats, Messrs A. P. Watt & Son and Messrs Macmillan for permission to quote from Yeats's poems and prose; to Mrs Yeats for permission to print four unpublished letters from Yeats to the author, and to Mrs Yeats and Michael Yeats for permission to include family portraits and to quote from letters written to the author by Elizabeth Corbet Yeats (Lolly) and Susan Mary Yeats (Lily); to the Chevalier Thomas McGreevy, Director of the National Gallery of Ireland, and to its Governors for permission to reproduce J. B. Yeats's portrait of Elizabeth C. Yeats; to the Department of External Affairs in Dublin for permission to reproduce the photographs of W. B. Yeats and Maud Gonne; and to Mrs Kingsmill Moore and Miss Winifred Letts for permission to print the caricature by Mac (Isabella Macnie).

The author would like to express his special thanks to Mrs Yeats. She has not seen this book, nor can she be expected to approve everything in it. But he wishes to place on record his profound admiration for the heroic devotion and understanding which she manifested towards the poet during his lifetime, and for her continued loyalty and service to the great heritage of his poetry since his death.

I

"I KNEW Willie Yeats when his trousers had fringes to them."

A massive, calm-visaged woman, sunk in the depths of a vast armchair, made this remark one night at Austin Clarke's, and for a moment I conjured up a picture of some curious period fashion, or a personal eccentricity like Wilde's knee-breeches, or the sashes of the young men who defended *Hernani*. Then it dawned on me that she meant she had known Yeats when the leanness of the family purse showed in the frayed ends of cloth above his shoe-laces.

Between that Yeats and the Yeats I knew, the Yeats of the brown evening shoes with great silver buckles, of the ribboned pince-nez and the hierarchic manner, lay half a lifetime of literary endeavour. By the time I met him he had fulfilled his ambitions.

> "The work is done," grown old he thought,
> "According to my boyish plan;
> Let the fools rage, I swerved in naught,
> Something to perfection brought;"
> *But louder sang that ghost, "What then?"*

Success was his: only the Greek philosopher came sometimes to his elbow to qualify that sense of achievement which was reflected in all he said or did. Yeats's manner was unique. He was the poet militant, conscious always of his vocation, and expecting everyone else to be conscious of it too. To the young and overawed he seemed the apotheosis of literary fame, not so much a man as a mask, a hierophant with a ritual for every phrase and action. His

11

human side, if he had one, was reserved for a few intimates. But for those who expected the poet, the poet assuredly was there, haughty, arrogant, oracular, absent-minded to the point almost of pose. He had shaped his literary personality so deliberately that it seemed to have taken over control and expelled the natural man. There could hardly be a greater contrast to the affectionate, lovable humility of de la Mare, or to the later, almost episcopal, friendliness of T. S. Eliot. Yeats's warring nature had carried him from one metamorphosis to another, and even those friends who had known him in youth give the impression of having grasped only a shadow.

It was easy to know the poems. It was more difficult, if not impossible, to know the man. The poems were my friends. Their cadenced harmony was a stately language to lull the spirit. But the man, when I met him, suggested harshness and scorn. The poems, then, are the essential prelude to anything I have to say about the man. In them was a quintessence, a highly aromatic distillation of a personality I had yet to meet,

I had been introduced to them by his sisters, who came to live in my father's parish of Dundrum in 1903. Neither Lolly nor Lily was then a churchgoer; the influence of free-thinking old John Butler Yeats may have kept them away. But by the time I was old enough to go to church they had both become regular attendants. They sat in a pew in the side-aisle, under the south gallery, slightly ahead of the rectory pew, and I regarded them with considerable interest. With the infallible instinct of the child I sensed that they were slightly different from the usual run of kindly supporters of parochial activity, in wide Edwardian hats, who gushed over one at the annual missionary bazaar.

Lolly Yeats ran a brushwork class on Saturday morning, which my elder sister, aged eight, attended. I, at six, was considered too young to go. At the class one painted endless snowdrops upon brown paper, which were afterwards

12

carried home and shown with great pride to one's relatives. Five smudges of Chinese white, together with a stalk of green, made a snowdrop; if the snowdrop was closed it was even easier; one smudge was then enough. It seemed to me that my abilities would be fully equal to this task.

I was bitterly envious; but my turn presently came. When I was twelve Lily Yeats sent my father a wall-card of "Innisfree," with illuminated capitals and framed with narrow, black adhesive tape. It was for me. She wrote: "I hear that young Willie is following in the steps of his cousin and has begun to write poetry. I want you to give him this."

It always amused me that the two sisters should call themselves our cousins. She was "Miss Yeats." They were "the Miss Yeatses." I knew who our cousins were: the Stubbs in Hatch Street, the O'Morchoes who filled Kilternan Rectory and succeeded us as visitors to my grandmother in August—they were wild and woolly, whereas we, according to my aunt, were nurse-ridden and starched—the Merediths who lived in Fitzwilliam Square, and the other Merediths in Wilton Terrace and in Baggot Street. More than this there could not be, since the available supply of aunts and uncles with children had already been exhausted.

Nevertheless the Yeatses were our cousins in the sense in which cousinship is still understood in tribal Ireland. All my letters from the two sisters or from Jack Yeats are signed "your affectionate cousin." The poet's great-grand-father, the Rev. John Yeats, rector of Drumcliff, had a sister, Mary Yeats, who was my great-great-grand-mother. There was a further relationship in the next generation, when a Terry married a Taylor, and a number of my letters from Lily Yeats are on genealogical matters, for she encouraged me to take an interest in our common ancestors.

If I had lived even one generation earlier I should not have thought her claim to cousinship so strange; for there were plenty of contacts then with various branches of the Yeats family. Some of these my father still kept up—Ellie

13

Yeats, Isaac Yeats. John Butler Yeats, when he married in 1864, lived in Sandymount Avenue, quite near the house of my great-grandfather. The latter must have been one of the first people to see the future poet abroad in his pram. Jack Yeats once told me how his father used to walk into Dublin every day with my grandfather, who was then a student at Trinity College. On the way they invariably met a red-haired woman. One morning, when my grandfather had to sit for an examination, he insisted on taking a different route. He dared not risk the ill-luck which such an encounter might bring him.

My cousin had sent me a wall-card, and up it went on my bedroom wall, to be a solace for many years to come. It did not threaten my allegiance to Wordsworth, which was already fanatical. It was of too different a kind. I liked it then; I like it still: for "Innisfree" lies outside the power of time. A. E. once warned Frank O'Connor that our pleasure in any work of art is finite. We should be on our guard against familiarity. With each reading of a poem its impact is slightly lessened. But "Innisfree" is one of those poems which give the lie to every stricture. Probably only one man has ever tired of it, and that was the man who wrote it. "I think," says Dorothy Wellesley, "he hated all his early poems, and Innisfree most of all. But one evening I begged him to read it. A look of tortured irritation came into his face, and continued there until the reading was over." It is hard to understand how he could have turned against it. The slow lilt of its rhythm moves with the nonchalance of French rather than of English verse; it suggests Lamartine's

"*Je promène au hasard mes regards sur la plaine*"

or Rimbaud's

"*Par les soirs bleus d'été j'irai dans les sentiers.*"

The poem had no forerunner, except a phrase from the

14

parable of the prodigal son; and it has no posterity, even in the poet's own work. Its naïve simplicity, its slightly uneven, almost ambling pace, the cadenced deliberation of each line, its vowel-music, although Yeats vowed that when he wrote it he scarcely knew what a vowel was, all make it unforgettable; a poem in which we can take refuge from every hardship of circumstance and outrage of time.

II

THE gift of the wall-card was followed by many other kindnesses. What was charming about the sisters was that they made you feel they took your literary ambitions seriously. You were one of the fraternity, even though you were only a round-faced schoolboy wearing tweed breeches buttoned at the knee. The greater part of their lives had been spent encouraging the aspirations of the male members of their family; an impecunious barrister father, suddenly turned portrait-painter; a brother dedicated to poetry from childhood; another brother determined to be a serious painter, but not too proud to earn five shillings with drawings for *Comic Cuts*. This art of ministering to talent unrecognised had passed into their nature. So now their manner towards a shy thirteen-year-old was subtly reassuring. It fell upon the spirit like gentle rain.

It became my habit to watch from the rectory window every Sunday morning about eleven o'clock until I saw Lily emerge onto the cabstand by the station from the Rat Hole (a name we had given to the cobbled tunnel for pedestrians under the railway line). Then I would hasten down the avenue and accompany her up the road to church. She was a slow walker. The bell was ringing, and it added a certain amount of excitement to our promenade to know that it might stop at any moment. In the same way, after church, I would wait for her by the side-door, and we would walk back slowly as far as the rectory gate.

Both the sisters were immensely proud of their poet brother. He had entered his forties now, and his reputation

16

LILY

was firmly established. Soon I would possess a copy of the *Poems* bound in jet-black calf, with a bright red-and-gilt spine, part of the Archbishop of Dublin's Literature Prize at my school. Such recognition in pedagogic circles would have amused the poet. Some of the critics had been slow enough to admit his merit. In Jersey, years later, I came across an old bound copy of *McClure's Magazine* and found among its book-reviews one headed "A Very Minor Poet Indeed." It was about the very collection that I was to receive from the episcopal hands, and it began with a direct insult: "Mr Yeats, in a volume under the misleading title of *Poems* . . ." After this contemptuous opening it went on to castigate the contents with considerable venom, holding up to particular scorn what seemed to the critic a trivial and absurd lyric beginning "Down by the salley gardens," a lyric which has since delighted thousands of readers and evoked one of the most successful musical settings of the poet's work.

I belonged to a younger generation, and "Down by the Salley Gardens" had had no novelty or strangeness for me. Already I was a Yeats fan. 'Innisfree' had been joined by another wall-card, purchased out of my pocket-money:

> Out-worn heart, in a time out-worn,
> Come clear of the nets of wrong and right;
> Laugh, heart, again in the grey twilight,
> Sigh, heart, again in the dew of the morn.

> Thy mother Eri is always young . . .

Here was all the glamour of the undefined. Sense or separate sentiment mattered hardly at all. I had discovered a poet who was the high priest of sound. Who was Eri? Why should God stand winding his lonely horn, like Roland over his unconscious warriors? Why should hope seem less dear than the dew of morn? It was all irrelevant. Unlike my well-loved Wordsworth this was someone to be heeded through the ear and not the mind.

A. E. said of his friend's earlier work: "I feel I am breathing in a divinely created nature, air, earth, the stars, ourselves, all fondled by the Magician of the Beautiful, all sharing in the benediction." And the enchantment is worked with so little. The mere tone of the words is enough.

> Time drops in decay,
> Like a candle burnt out,
> And the mountains and woods
> Have their day, have their day;
> What one in the rout
> Of the fire-born moods
> Has fallen away?

Poem after poem fixed itself firmly in my consciousness. Yeats could take a phrase as banal as "But think about old friends the most," and, by giving it a purely personal inflection, could weave it into one of his most moving lyrics:

> Though you are in your shining days,
> Voices among the crowd
> And new friends busy with your praise,
> Be not unkind or proud,
> But think about old friends the most:
> Time's bitter flood will rise,
> Your beauty perish and be lost
> For all eyes but these eyes.

One would have to be deaf, or wholly insensible, not to respond to heard and half-heard melodies as sweet as these. Poems like "The Stolen Child" and the ballads, which Lily expected me to enjoy, were soon elbowed into second place. Instead I chanted, like Wandering Aengus:

> Though I am old with wandering
> Through hollow lands and hilly lands,
> I will find out where she has gone,
> And kiss her lips and take her hands;
> And walk among long dappled grass,
> And pluck till time and times are done
> The silver apples of the moon,
> The golden apples of the sun.

My contacts with the Yeats sisters multiplied. Of the two Lolly was the livelier, the more volatile, the more talkative. But Lily—there is a magnificent portrait of her by her father in the National Gallery of Ireland—was in some ways better company. She was the favourite, both with John Butler Yeats and with W. B. The women of that family had been sacrificed to its men. Hone implies that it was almost a relief to the mother, after two strokes, to retire to a life entirely in one room, "forgetful at last of money troubles, occasionally able to read a little, never allowing it to be said that she was an invalid, and finding happiness in feeding the birds at her window." She died in 1900, and about two years later John Butler Yeats gave up the house in Bedford Park in London and came with his daughters to Dundrum. Lily from her portrait was a fine-looking, brown-eyed, intelligent young woman with an air of sleepy grace, and she remained handsome to the end of her life. I never heard of her having had any admirer. Their mother's illness, her death, their father's dependence upon them, may have ruled out all idea of marriage. In those days daughters were expected to sacrifice themselves.

Family life may have been financially anxious, but it was never, I feel sure, either dull or dour. I have a number of tiny, coloured, comic drawings by Jack Yeats which Lily, a few years before her death, cut out of her journal and sent to me. They are concerned with the adventures of an imaginary character, Theo, invented by Jack and the poet Masefield. Theo is a buccaneer and always in trouble. On one occasion he has to disguise himself as a young lady and is shown lacing himself into his corset. Sketched from time to time, as the spirit moved Jack, into his sister's diary, the drawings give an idea of the spirit of fun and the friendly relations in the Yeats home. Hone speaks of the lifelong friendship between W. B. and Lily, "without a single quarrel between them once the schoolroom was left aside." This single reservation is supported by what an old governess of

19

the Yeats children once told my sister: "Everything used to go splendidly in the nursery until Willie came home. Then the quarrelling began immediately."

Sometimes I accompanied Lily to a matinée at the Abbey Theatre. I was really the poet's guest. It was he, she explained, who arranged for a couple of complimentary tickets to be sent to her from time to time. We would meet at Dundrum station, take the train to Harcourt Street and descend the long flight of steps to the street below. Lily was in her forties at this time and already moved with the deliberation of middle age. She and her youthful cavalier would proceed by tram as far as Sackville Street and then walk slowly down Abbey Street to the theatre.

Our seats were invariably in the third row of the stalls, and as we waited for the play to begin she would regale me with tidbits of information; where W. B. found the great gong which sounded at the beginning of each act; what sequence of chance circumstances had led to the discovery of a particular actor or actress; or who that very tall and thin young man with pince-nez was, who had just gone up the short flight of steps at the side of the orchestra.

Once she even took me up the steps and through the doorway at the top, and we made our way to the Green Room, where two cups of tea were produced, and I listened for the first time to the good-natured chatter of that heroic profession which feels an obligation to present a brave outward show to the world through all vicissitudes. The Abbey was my introduction to Synge's work. I saw a superb performance of *The Well of the Saints*. I saw and laughed at Lady Gregory's *Damer's Gold*. At *The King's Threshold* I was duly moved by the fine poetic defiance of Seanchan in the face of the High King's threats, and still more moved, if the truth be known, by the long fair hair falling about the face of the very beautiful young actress who took the part of Fedelm. I still remember her flowing tresses, but I have forgotten her name.

20

It shocked me that Seanchan could rage against anyone so lovely.

> Go where you will,
> So it be out of sight and out of mind.
> I cast you from me like an old torn cap,
> A broken shoe, a glove without a finger,
> A crooked penny; whatever is most worthless.

The everyday speech of the Elizabethans was rhetorical, and therefore rhetoric remained realistic in the mouths of their actors. But the stage rhetoric of the late nineteenth century had no relation to contemporary speech. Yeats's dramatic iambics seem to me, now, no better than those of Tennyson. They are so obviously a literary device contrived by someone who has first put on his singing robes.

> The sword is in the rope—
> The rope's in two—it falls into the sea,
> It whirls into the foam. O ancient worm,
> Dragon that loved the world and held us to it,
> You are broken, you are broken. The world
>   drifts away,
> And I am left alone with my beloved,
> Who cannot put me from his sight for ever.*

This is the sort of thing that any poet can turn out by the hundred yards, if he gives his mind to it, and no matter how well spoken on the stage, it remains divorced from life.

* *The Shadowy Waters.*

21

III

YEATS's plays have lost their hold over me, but the mesmeric power of his prose has not yet waned. Even as a schoolboy I could not read ten lines of it without passing immediately beneath its spell. It is pontifical, transmuting even the most ordinary statements.

When we were children we did not say at such a distance from the post-office, or so far from the butcher's or the grocer's, but measured things by the covered well in the wood, or by the burrow of the fox in the hill.

This is as sonorous as Ruskin, although the subject-matter may be trivial. The early prose—of *The Celtic Twilight*—is mannered, but at the same time charming. In *The Trembling of the Veil* Yeats writes with humour and an occasionally distressing realism. But in the later prose he reverts again to an impressive and mysterious gravity which sometimes becomes pompous. All the Yeats family had a flair for recreating an occasion and for remembering the vivid phrase, a trait which comes out in the titles to Jack's pictures, which are almost poems in themselves. The poet will slip into his argument the wonderful remark made to him by a young girl—too young, he says, to realise the profundity of her observation—"Innocence is the highest achievement of the intelligence." Or he will draw what Katharine Tynan considered an idealised portrait of her father but yet keep all the essential flavour of the old farmer.

Yeats's prose is perhaps at his best when he is defending his own vocation. Then he speaks with passion and eloquence:

The arts have failed; fewer people are interested in them every generation. The mere business of living, of making money, of amusing oneself, occupies people more and more, and makes them less and less capable of the difficult art of appreciation. When they buy a picture it generally shows a long-current idea, or some conventional form that can be admired in that lax mood one admires a fine carriage or fine horses in; and when they buy a book it is so much in the manner of the picture that it is forgotten, when its moment is over, as a glass of wine is forgotten. We who care deeply about the arts find ourselves the priesthood of an almost forgotten faith, and we must, I think, if we would win the people again, take upon ourselves the method and the fervour of a priesthood. We must be half humble and half proud.

Even when treating the simplest theme Yeats hangs a curtain between himself and the commonplace. But as the Chinese say, "one cannot remain forever standing on tiptoe," and the cumulative effect of this dignity of approach sometimes becomes pretentious.

Those who write today treat prose solely as a means of communication. Yeats treated it as incantation, although he was completely unmusical. There have been successful ballet dancers who had practically no feeling for music and who had to count their steps carefully. In the same way Yeats, whose ear for words was so perfect, was tone-deaf, and could not recognise the simplest tune. The music of his poetry is partly vowel-music and partly derived from his sense of pace. He is a master of pace.

Fasten your hair with a golden pin.

Be you still, be you still, trembling heart.

Who dreamed that beauty passes like a dream?

I wander by the edge
Of this desolate lake.

23

Do you not hear me calling, white deer with no horns?

All the heavy days are over;
Leave the body's coloured pride.

Down by the salley gardens my love and I did meet.

In every one of these the pace is different, although a similar aura of magic hangs about them all.

Even his use of names seems based on music.

Caolte tossing his burning hair,
And Niamh calling *Away, come away.*

One of his poems reached me often, at this time, with its easy and flowing rhythms already stressed by the appropriate notes. Living near us in Sydenham Road, where Yeats was later to live for a time, were the Pigotts. The daughter Helen, a girl of nineteen or twenty, was dark-haired and creamy-complexioned, with the face of a madonna and the slow easy movements of the priestess of some Burmese temple. She had a very beautiful contralto voice greatly in demand at parish concerts and drawing-room parties. The songs which she sang were mostly sentimental period pieces like "Absent" and "Because," but sooner or later she would be asked for "Had I the heavens' embroidered cloths," not in the setting most widely known but in another and, I would say, more beautiful one. It was phrased in what was then a modern musical idiom, as vague and wandering as Delius or Debussy, but it moved slowly towards a most magnificent climax. Even my untutored ears waited eagerly for that moment when, with absolute certitude, her voice would flow out, freely and easily, in that last line of superb and nostalgic melody:

Tread softly because you tread on my dreams.

There were poems which needed no music. The simplicity of

She carries in the dishes,
And lays them in a row.

24

> To an isle in the water
> With her would I go.

is almost monosyllabic. I read other poets for what they
said, but even as a schoolboy I read Yeats for the way in
which he said it. I was a susceptible youth and the love
poems seemed like a personal revelation. I knew well
already that love was a delicious uneasiness of the spirit. I
knew that part of its anguish was its uncertainty. One was
liable to suspect a conspiracy on the part of the whole
universe to prevent one seeing the beloved, say, at the
particular children's party at which one had hoped to see
her. I knew, furthermore, that one would like to protect
her from all the slings and arrows of outrageous fortune, but
that actually there was nothing to be done except to wait in
a state of trembling anticipation, which was half fear, for the
moment when one would be once more reassured of her real
existence. All this I knew; but how wonderful to have it
brought home to me more forcibly than ever in these lines:

> A pity beyond all telling
> Is hid in the heart of love:
> The folk who are buying and selling,
> The clouds on their journey above,
> The cold wet winds ever blowing,
> And the shadowy hazel grove
> Where mouse-grey waters are flowing,
> Threaten the head that I love.

In a string hammock, slung between two sycamore trees,
I devoured the slim volumes as they came successively
from the Cuala Press. My father subscribed for them, but
it was I who seized them and carried them off to the garden
to read first, after they had been delivered by hand by one
of the work-girls. It was no longer the Dun Emer Press:
it had been rechristened when they moved to Churchtown.
There, in a small, picturesque, red-brick building called
Rose Cottage, opposite a dairy-farmer's field, the two
sisters carried on their printing and embroidery. Lily and

25

her helpers plied their needles in one room; in another stood the little eighteenth-century hand-press, while all round the walls hung various of its products, illuminated wall-cards, hand-coloured prints of pictures by Jack Yeats, broadsides. Each month for six or seven years a new broadside appeared, furbished with vivid, coloured illustrations by Jack. As well, two books came every year from the press, on handmade paper and in an edition of anything from two hundred and fifty to four hundred copies. A tail-piece in red lettering gave the date on which the printing was finished:

Here ends Poems and Translations by John M. Synge, Poet and Dramatist, who died on the twenty-fourth day of March, nineteen hundred and nine. This book has been printed and published by Elizabeth C. Yeats at the Cuala Press, Church-town, Dundrum and finished on the eighth day of April of the same year. The book had been in the press as Synge lay dying, and Yeats's preface to it is dated 4 April, only four days before the printing was completed.

W. B. was the director of all the press's literary activities. He had made Macmillan concede the right to print these semi-private pre-editions, so that his sisters might make some money out of his work. He was not always easy to collaborate with. Lolly might speak of him jocularly, but it was the sort of jocularity with which frail mortals refer to Jove, an overlord guilty sometimes of absurdities, but capable also of wielding thunderbolts in a highly awkward way. If, on some very rare occasion, she remarked "Willie was here the other day," it was abundantly clear that the Cuala dovecot was only just beginning to recover from the flutter into which he had thrown it.

I remember being invited by Lolly to come to Rose Cottage and see the Cuala Industries at work. In their long dark-blue overalls the sisters and the half-dozen girls who worked for them suggested the William Morris period. This was appropriate enough, for it was May Morris, the

LOLLY

poet's daughter, who had taught Lily to embroider. Not that there was anything arty-crafty about Lily, and still less about Lolly who had a cheerful, forceful air of continual endeavour. Jack was the quietest of the family, Lolly the most loquacious. She rattled on brightly on all occasions, hindered only slightly by a mannerism which gave the impression that she had a hot potato in her mouth. Her volubility ignored the potato and may indeed have been the explanation of it. There was something heroic about Lolly's jaunty talkativeness, and about Lily's gentle and reassuring calm, for they had both known for years what most people find agonising and even demoralising, the continual strain of financial stringency.

They lived about a mile from Rose Cottage, in a small two-storey house known as Ghurteen Dhas. There they were tended by a devoted family servant, in fact two when I first knew them. This may sound plutocratic, but in those days a servant could be had for twelve pounds a year or less.

Lolly showed me everything at Rose Cottage with pride and with her customary brusque liveliness. A bronze dragon surmounted the small printing press, a girl was at work pressing down the handle and stripping off the sheets and I was sent away with a proof copy of one publication, Masefield's essay on Synge, with the top right-hand corner of each page torn off so that it could not possibly be confused with any of the numbered issue, a mutilation which slightly shocked the bibliophile in me but did not detract from my pleasure in owning the book.

I had the friendliest contacts with Yeats's two sisters, though I had not yet set eyes on the poet himself. These were years when Ireland did not see a great deal of him. He might come to Coole Park in the summer to Lady Gregory, and when she and Lennox Robinson took over the tour of the Abbey players in America in 1911 Yeats had to return to supervise the second company in Dublin for the greater part of the winter of 1911–12.

It is likely therefore that it was then that I saw him for the first time. I was with my father in Dublin one day. We had just come to the top of Abbey Street, and were about to turn into what was then still Sackville Street, when we passed a tall, stoutish man in a wide-brimmed, almost "wild west" grey felt hat, and wearing a floppy, transparent, blue silk tie, tied in an enormous bow. As soon as we had passed him my father said in a low voice, "That was your cousin, the poet Yeats."

I looked quickly back. The poet had been walking along slowly in a mood of abstraction so deliberate as almost to appear self-conscious. It was as though he demanded notice and at the same time repudiated it. He had come to a halt now on the edge of the curb, and, in some curious way, he seemed at once aware and unaware of the fact that a belted, tweed-suited schoolboy was staring at him. Yeats always seemed to know when eyes were upon him, and to plan his mannerisms accordingly. But in fact he was very short-sighted, so that this may not have been the case at all.

He stood now at the street-corner as though trying hard to recollect where he was going, or whether he was going anywhere at all. The general impression was a little disappointing. He was too plump, too podgy, and the broad black riband trailing from his pince-nez, as well as the huge bow tie falling into his waistcoat, savoured of affectation. The Augustus John portrait in *Collected Poems* suggests the man I saw, and in it the silk bow is even larger and less controlled. Lennox Robinson had met him not long before and describes him as slim; but he hastens to add, "I have said that when I met him first he was slim; that was not always the case. He could vary, and very rapidly, from leanness to stoutness. I used to tell him that he was like the moon that waxed and waned." It is clear which phase of the moon I had encountered.

Nevertheless, there he was, the poet himself, and my heart beat slightly faster. It did not strike me as strange

28

that my father had not exchanged any greeting with his cousin. I seldom heard any reference made to the poet in my home, and only a very occasional one to his artist father.

My own father was a wide reader and lover of poetry, and amongst the many sermons in his Bible I find one entitled "Innisfree." But I imagine he found it a good deal easier to chat with free-thinking old John Butler Yeats—to whom in later life he bore a distinct facial resemblance, noticed by Lily and others—than with his curious and occult-minded son. Families tend, in any case, to be grudging in their appreciation of a blood-relative, and the hackles of the latter rise instinctively at the approach of the consanguineous, knowing that this latent hostility exists. Yeats was accepted in my home as a poet who had actually managed to make good, a feat which, like that of the man who swallows half a dozen nails and a two-edged dagger, instinctively commands our respect. But at the same time I sensed dimly that he was regarded as slightly over-estimating his own importance in the world. It may have been my mother who gave me the impression that he was a "queer fish," and this was further strengthened by the tone of awe in which his own sisters spoke of him. Obviously the great man was not a person to be trifled with.

Although W. B. was seldom discussed, Shaw became frequently the subject of conversation. G. B. S. had been recognised early in his career as the arch-enemy of all the conventions and reticences. One Sunday a visiting preacher was lunching with us after church. Suddenly I pricked up my ears. The conversation had become interesting. The visitor said that if Yeats and Shaw were asked to assess their own merits in relation to Shakespeare, Shaw would undoubtedly say "Shaw, Shakespeare, Yeats;" whereas Yeats would at least have the modesty to make it "Shakespeare, Yeats, Shaw." This was received with a burst of laughter and cordial endorsement. All the same it had been made very clear that Yeats's modesty was only relative.

29

IV

THE Yeats whom I saw standing vaguely at the corner of Abbey Street was a man of forty-five or more. At least four different phases of his life were already behind him—the retiring boy, the romantic idealist, the conqueror of London drawing-rooms, and the fighter who had carried the Abbey Theatre venture to a successful issue. He had come far and passed through various stages. In 1872, when the boy was only seven, we find John Butler Yeats writing from London to his wife in Sligo:

I am very anxious about Willy, he is never out of my thoughts. I believe him to be intensely affectionate, but from shyness, sensitiveness and nervousness, difficult to win and yet he is worth winning. I should of course like to see him do what is right but he will only develop by kindness and affection and gentleness . . . Bobby is robust and hardy and does not mind rebuffs—but Willy is sensitive, intellectual and emotional, very easily rebuffed and continually afraid of being rebuffed, so that with him one has to use sensitiveness which is so rare at Merville . . . I wish greatly Willy could be made more robust by riding or other means—*not by going to school.* I was very sorry he could not have the pony more.

When I came to know her I used to question Katharine Tynan about W. B.'s youth.

"What was he like? Was he as picturesque as the Sargent drawing? Were you in love with him?" I once asked her.

"I can't imagine any woman being in love with the young Willie Yeats."

She proceeded to describe a moist-handed, shy youth,

30

quite incapable of inspiring passion. When A. E. came to tea with me in Swanage a year or two before his death, he told me, among other recollections of their joint boyhood, the story of W. B.'s proposal to Katie. His father remarked to him one day, "Willie, you've been seeing a lot of that girl. It is time that you proposed." So Willie dutifully made his way out to the Tynans' farm near Tallaght and offered his hand and heart to Katie. It was refused. Whereupon, his manner indicating some slight relief, Katharine Tynan asked him, "But why did you do this?" "Well, my father thought——" and the whole story came out.

This may have been apocryphal fancy on A. E.'s part, but it matches well enough with the portrait that she draws in her memoirs. There he is "very simple, passionately generous to his friends, absorbed in his art."

Looking back [she says], it seems to me that there was something almost pathetic about him. He was so gentle, so eager to do what one wanted, so patient when one drove him hither and thither. He was made happy by so little kindness. . . . He was most adaptable in a household; for he never cared what he ate or drank, or in what corner he slept, nor what he did for the matter of that, so long as there was someone to talk poetry with him. When he stayed with us and wanted to go to town, he was quite ready to take a seat with Tommy Merrigan who drove a milk-van into town. The spectacle of the poet sitting up among the milk-cans is a weird one in my memory. Other young gentlemen occasionally accepted a seat in the milk-van, taking care to get off before they reached the parts of the city that counted. Not so the poet, who would drive through the smartest streets in the milk-van, unconscious or careless that it differed from the finest carriage.

The boy on the milk-cart became the darling of the London drawing-rooms and the man who could seem arrogant even to some of his oldest friends. Katharine Tynan hints as much; but at the same time she claims that she had "a bit of him which no one else has." She and George Russell had known him in the earliest days of his

31

inspiration and they never forgot that vivid and miracle-
working creature.

"The Yeats of the Irish Theatre," she wrote, "and of
much petting and spoiling is, or may be, quite a different
person. The Yeats of that time—well, I knew more about
him than anyone else outside his own family; and I feel
that I keep him as he was in those days." It was this early
Yeats whom A. E. remembered all his life, the black-haired
youth who used to sit with him—so Lily once told me—in
the basement kitchen, long after the rest of the family had
gone to bed, debating what magnetic force it was that made
the mushrooms grow.

Personality passes through a whole succession of aspects.
The world leaves its scars on most men. The "eager and
fervid" boy became the aloof stranger, and, presently, the
angry and scornful old man. Katharine Tynan blames his
plunging into public affairs. She utters "a malediction upon
the Irish Theatre which could have dispensed quite well with
the sacrifice of what was given for the supreme delight of
mankind." Entrance into the fray may have roughened a
sensitive nature, for the sensitive can survive only by har-
dening their own nature. But that cannot have been the
whole explanation. Whatever the causes, contradiction and
stress were there. An eagle tore at the liver of this Prome-
theus of words.

The beribboned figure pointed out to me by my father
was still unmarried. Three or four years later, in 1914, he
was still apologising to his ancestors:

> Pardon that for a barren passion's sake,
> Although I have come close on forty-nine,
> I have no child, I have nothing but a book,
> Nothing but that to prove your blood and mine.

He was a bachelor of nearly fifty by then. Maud Gonne
had rejected him as both husband and lover. Mrs Olivia
Shakespear may have proved kinder. But the circumstances
of his life had left their mark on the man. One cannot

32

imagine a greater contrast in character than the two brothers. Jack was the younger of the two and had been perhaps less conscious of the financial stresses of the Yeats home, and the snubs that had helped to give W. B. his *hauteur*. In any case his nature was altogether sweeter, so that he would not have minded them. He was disposed to find people kindly and to think life good fun. And he had no need to apologise to his ancestors for being still unmarried at forty-nine. Contrariwise he had married very young. Lily Yeats once told me how Jack, while still working in the art school, had found himself sitting next a fellow-student, pleasing to the eye and of sympathetic outlook. He used to return home to receive his father's periodic enquiry "And how is Dottie?" "*Cottie*, not Dottie, please, Father." It was a long time before his parent could get it right. But Jack had married his Cottie, while they were still art students, and they had begun their long life of mutual devotion, a highly successful alliance which allowed Jack's gentle disposition to remain unspoiled.

W. B. was to make a successful and happy marriage also, but late in life. He was to marry a woman who would be the loyal and perfect companion. But before he did so, there was to be the curious incident of his proposal to Maud Gonne's daughter, Iseult. That he should have been in love with the mother, and then wished, years later, to marry the daughter, has almost the tang of a Maupassant story. And, by a further coincidence, the drama was staged in Maupassant's native Normandy.

In 1916 Maud Gonne's husband, Major MacBride, from whom she had been separated for a number of years, was executed after the rising. She sent Yeats a message in London by her daughter that she was "very sad" and "lonely" and the poet went to Normandy where she was living, contemplating marriage with her, now that she was free, but having first made a compact with Lady Gregory that for the sake of the Abbey Theatre he would not marry Maud Gonne unless she gave up politics. Marriage was discussed between them when he got to France, but, as Hone puts it, "she was far more interested in securing a passport to Ireland to work for the prisoners than in any such notion."

What happened then is admirably told in Hone's pages and intelligible enough in the circumstances. Yeats had listened to Iseult Gonne's praises from his London friends, and to Lady Cunard exclaiming "Never in my life have I seen such a complexion." He was deputed now to bring her back to Normandy and wrote to Lady Gregory, "She makes me sad, for I think that if my life had been normal I might have had a daughter of her age." There followed a long succession of weeks in that strange household in France, with the young girl acting as the poet's secretary. In a letter to Lady Gregory he says: "I am really managing Iseult very well. The other night she made a prolonged appeal for an extra cigarette. . . . I have stayed on much longer than I intended but I think you will forgive me under the circumstances—as father, but as father only, I have been a great success." He went away but returned in the summer of 1917 and, Hone tells us, "repeated a proposal of marriage." He was refused. "I don't think she will change her mind, she has not the impulse to marry. We take long walks—she shows me many little signs of affection but otherwise things are as I wrote." His proposal to Iseult made Maud Gonne unhappy. It was of Iseult he had written, when she was still a child:

> O you will take whatever's offered
> And dream that all the world's a friend,
> Suffer as your mother suffered,
> Be as broken in the end.
> But I am old and you are young,
> And I speak a barbarous tongue.

Yeats secured passports and travelled back to England with them. They were searched at Southampton for secret

34

codes, while Yeats fumed up and down the platform. And in London Maud Gonne was served with an order under D.O.R.A. forbidding her to proceed to Ireland. She took a flat in Chelsea and Denison Ross found Iseult a post as assistant librarian in the School of Oriental Languages, whereupon, Hone tells us, the poet burst into tears from sheer relief, one more indication of the strength of his feelings.

I had left school and was in France myself at the moment when all this was happening, not so many kilometres away. I had gone out to France in July 1916, after only three months' training in England, a very youthful subaltern in a horse transport company, first down on the Somme, then up near Béthune; and then, later, with our horse-lines on Vimy Ridge itself. The days were gone when I had lain in the rectory hammock cutting the pages of the just-received Cuala *Responsibilities*, and puzzled by the couplet from Khoung-fou-tseu which prefaced it:

> How am I fallen from myself, for a long time now
> I have not seen the Prince of Chang in my dreams.

For a long time now I had been a stranger to that safe, sleepy, pre-war world in which books mattered more than anything else. Not that I had ceased to care for them. My valise was laden down with them. In a rest billet of one night's duration at St Venant I found myself sleeping for the first time in months in a bed with sheets, and celebrated the occasion by taking out Seumas O'Sullivan's *Poems* from my kit-bag and re-reading them in these surroundings of relative luxury. I had no Yeats with me, but one of my first acts, on finding myself in the possession of corps pay at the rate of seven shillings a day, had been to write to my bookseller friend, Neale, on Aston Quay, and tell him I wanted to buy the eight-volume vellum-backed Shakespeare Head collected Yeats, which had come into the market at a slightly reduced price, when Bullen got into financial difficulties. I had seen it with envy often in his shop. Now I was actually in a position to purchase it.

From France I wrote presently to my father to ask him to leave the first volume of the eight with Lily Yeats, who was to ask the poet to sign it for me, when she next saw him. When I returned to Dublin in September 1917 to begin nearly a year of life in army hospitals, convalescent homes and command depots, the volume had been duly signed and returned to my father.

I opened it eagerly and was a little taken aback by the brief inscription in tiny, spidery writing on the blank page inside the cover. It was so minute that one had difficulty in reading it. The poet had written:

> I have heard the pigeons of the Seven Woods
> Make their faint thunder.
>
> W. B. Yeats. July 5 1957.

What, I wondered, had made him write that? Had he been told by Lily that I was in the army, and had he guessed that, at the moment when he was writing it, I was listening to the sound of sixteen-inch shells bursting either side of the Arras-Mont St Eloi road, and watching the huge mushrooms of earth and debris flung up by them as they did so? My life was a very safe affair compared to that of an average infantryman. Nevertheless I had had to ride with my wagons up past the railway embankment in front of Arras, before the attack on Oppy Wood, and had seen our guns, massed wheel to wheel, sending a barrage over our heads, and had heard such a thunder as all the pigeons of the world could not have made between them. I knew, too, that the faint murmur of pigeons in a wood is a more significant sound than that of any gunfire man could ever ingeniously devise, because it is the thunder of life, resurgent and joyful. And it occurred to me that the same thought must have been in W. B.'s mind when he chose his quotation.

36

He had signed my book, but it was several years before I was to meet him personally. This is all the stranger because in 1919 he rented a house in Sydenham Road, Dundrum, only a few hundred yards from the gate of the rectory. I had been invalided out of the army in September 1918, and in the following January went to Jersey on a farming course arranged by the Ministry of Pensions. But I came home every summer, and it would have been easy enough to have asked my father or Lily to make the introduction.

Yeats by now was married. He had married Miss Hyde-Lees at the Harrow Road registry office in London on 21 October 1917. She was to make him an heroic and devoted wife, maintaining her own personality despite the tremendous impact of his—which would have been overwhelming for most women—sharing in all his mental activities, giving him for the rest of his life the benefit of her loyalty and devotion, and serving his memory in countless ways after his death. A few weeks later he wrote to Lady Gregory, "My wife is a perfect wife, kind, wise, and unselfish. I think you were such another young girl once. She has made my life serene and full of order."

Hone does not mention their residence in Sydenham Road but I cannot have dreamt it, and Hone does speak of "various lodgings in the vicinity of Dublin." I am also under the impression that my father baptised one, if not both, of Yeats's children, though I seem to remember his saying that the christening took place in Donnybrook church. Certainly they met at this time, although I do not think that any real contact was established between them. My father was the friendliest of men, one at whose graveside as many Roman Catholics as Protestants are said to have stood, and on whose coffin, amidst all the many wreaths, rested a tiny bouquet of roadside flowers, gathered by the local roadsweeper, who whispered to my sister, "He never passed me on the road without a friendly word." Yeats on

37

the other hand was almost an anti-cleric. So, if any iron curtain dropped between the two men, it seems fairly certain that it was the poet and not the parson who dropped it. Some months later, when Yeats had moved to Oxford, Lolly told us how one of his children had been taken ill and the doctor had had to be smuggled into the house by a side-door and instructed beforehand that, if he encountered the poet on the stair, he was to pretend to be the electrician or the gas man. This lest he should rouse the poet's anxiety and thus spoil the flow of inspiration. To me this seemed a most wise and rational precaution. But it was clear that my mother, who had brought eight children into the world —the first five in far-off China—had no sympathy with a man whose poetic susceptibilities had to be considered in a moment of such domestic importance. And yet Yeats was conscious enough of his parental role. In *A Prayer for My Son* he voices the wish of all fathers of the newly born:

> And may departing twilight keep
> All dread afar till morning's back,
> That his mother may not lack
> Her fill of sleep.

V

I COULD, as I have said, have made Yeats's acquaintance when he lived in Dundrum, but I did not, for a number of reasons. I was absent most of the year in the Channel Islands, and when I returned on holiday there were many friends to see. But also at this time I tended to avoid literary contacts as too stimulating, too exciting, too exhausting. I had gone to the war very young, and looking still younger. A photograph of the time might be that of a boy of fifteen, and the first thing the Adjutant at Aldershot had said to me was "You look far too youthful. You must grow a moustache," a feat unfortunately beyond my powers. I came back from France in a mood akin to that of Siegfried Sassoon, disillusioned about the Allies' war aims, savagely indignant about their propaganda, and three if not four parts a disciple of Tolstoy. In the King George V Military Hospital at Arbour Hill, up by the Phoenix Park, my mind still tended to run on all these problems. I would go to a matinée of Shaw's *John Bull's Other Island* in the afternoon, and to Ibsen's *An Enemy of the People* that same evening, and would return to hospital with my brain in a ferment, full of contempt for and indignation against both the individual and society. A hurricane of ideas was the last thing I needed. I was in hospital to rest, but I ignored that consideration.

Eventually I learnt the hard way; and having learnt, went almost to the other extreme, and tried to avoid anything that could over-excite my mind. About 1920 G. K. Chesterton came to Ireland at the time of the Black and

39

Tans, and the Yeats sisters gave an evening party for him at Ghurteen Dhas. Lily invited me, but I refused the invitation. My brother-in-law Willie Jameson went, and, I think, my father, and from them I heard an account of the occasion. Feeling ran high at the moment, and, though Chesterton was a Liberal and wholly against the Black and Tans, he was too good an Englishman to accept all the strictures made that evening upon his country. There had been a tremendous dust-up between him and Ernest Boyd. It was still in progress when my brother-in-law left at midnight. In the hall he met Thomas Bodkin who was also slipping away. "Too much like a dog-fight!" was Bodkin's whispered comment, as he struggled into his coat in the narrow passage.

Though I denied myself the pleasure and excitement of the party, I was often at Ghurteen Dhas to drink a cup of tea and have a chat with Lily. The door would be opened by Rose—the same maid, I rather think, who years before had seen the schoolboy Russell pass the window early one morning and, before any of the family knew him, nicknamed him The Strayed Angel. The walls of the narrow passage were covered with pictures and photographs, and there was an oak chest in which Lily kept all her copies of the Cuala and Dun Emer books. On the left of the passage there were two sitting-rooms opening into one another, the farther one rather dark and both with every inch of wall-space covered either by books or by prints, photographs or paintings. There were portraits of the two sisters by their father, a photograph of the latter, white-bearded and trim, taken since he went to New York, early drawings and many prints by Jack Yeats, and a couple of early pictures by George Russell.

I would find Lily sometimes in one room and sometimes in the other. It must have been plain to her that it was distinctly exciting for me to sit there listening to her, asking questions about Synge and other celebrities, or to get up

40

and wander round the room, pulling out a book from the bookcase, or pausing in front of a particular picture. She was a restful person. Her father had found her restful, W. B. found her restful, and now, as she poured out tea and chatted away quietly, I too felt her calming influence. She had the family gift of giving point to a story by some turn of speech. They all had it, a relish for individual idiom, anything that gave a tang and a flavour to language, and it may have been this inherited trait that accounted in the first instance for the poet's fanatical zeal for the distinguished and original phrase.

Lily was not only restful, she was generous. She had another chest in the back sitting-room, full of souvenirs of the past. Sometimes Richard Best would come out from the National Library to take tea with her and she would open the chest and find him some early drawing of her father's for the archives of the National Library. Possibly Best purchased them on behalf of the Library, but I rather think that they were gifts. The drawing of W. B. as a boy, sprawled on a chair and reading a book, which has been reproduced on a postcard that you can purchase from the attendant at the National Library, came out of Lily's hoard, and I myself have three excellent pencil drawings by John Butler Yeats, given to me on three different occasions, to my great delight. Lily would wait till I was going and then go to the chest and begin searching in it. Presently she would find a sketch that she liked, torn out by the artist from one of his sketchbooks; after a last affectionate look at it she would say that she would like me to have it. One of the three given me is of Miss Horniman, patron of the Abbey Theatre. The other two are of agreeable-looking women whose names I have forgotten.

She gave me sketches, she lent me books, and—though she had no evidence to support the assumption—she reassured me immeasurably by taking it for granted that I too would one day see my name on the title-page of a book.

41

There was not yet much earnest for it. The quarterly *Studies* had published two or three poems that I had sent them; and presently the literary editor of the *Spectator*, St Loe Strachey's daughter, Amabel Williams-Ellis, would take some prose poems I had submitted ("a form I normally detest") and would print several of them in that journal. Courtney of the *Fortnightly Review* would go one better and accept a batch of twelve. These acceptances were signalised by the shedding of my first Christian name. The second—derived from the surname of a great-great-grandmother—had appeared in every generation since, and seemed more likely to stick in the memory of a reader. I became Monk Gibbon, which was to cause confusion to a number of people, Yeats among them, who had always heard me referred to as Willie Gibbon.

About this time too, on one of my periodic returns from Jersey, I summoned up courage and, knowing his reputation for kindness to the neophyte, sent A. E. a batch of poems and prose poems for criticism. They came back to me with a long, closely-written and extremely helpful letter, and I was invited to visit him at Plunkett House. I did so, had tea with him and Susan Mitchell, but did not avail myself of the invitation to go to Rathgar Avenue on Sunday evening. To my friends I seemed energetic, physically fit, a keen tennis-player and hockey-player; but the war had left mental scars, not visible on the hockey-field but very real, and late hours and literary conversation left me, to use a phrase W. B. had used in a letter to Katie Tynan yeats before, "sucked dry as an orange."

Yeats had taken a house in Oxford in October 1919 and he remained there for two years, happy enough in his contacts with the students, according to Hone, but according to Lily Yeats more and more irritated by an exclusively academic setting. When he returned to Ireland in 1922, having purchased a house in Merrion Square, Lily's story to me was that they now realised they had spent two years

HOW THE POETS PASSED

of increasing dissatisfaction in Oxford solely because of a misunderstanding. "George* says that she only went there to please W. B.; and W. B. says that he only went there because he thought that it would please George." In the event, I was given to understand, neither of them had been pleased.

No. 82 Merrion Square was to be a much more successful venture. It was only two doors away from Plunkett House where A. E. worked daily. Mac's famous cartoon shows the two great men passing one another in front of the intermediate No. 83, each completely oblivious of the other's presence, although they are on the way to visit one another. W. B. had accepted Cosgrave's offer of nomination to the Senate. He was a public figure in his own country, and the award of the Nobel Prize to him in 1923 symbolised his recognition as a world figure.

Lily told me that W. B. was at home to friends on Monday evenings and urged me to go. She promised to explain that I was coming. For a long time I did not adopt her suggestion. Finally I went in December 1923. A long letter next day to a friend in Jersey described the visit in detail, but the only record that I have now is one written ten months later in my journal and dated November 1924. It forms part of a discursive note on a number of Irish writers whom I had met by that time.

Yeats was now fifty-eight years old. The boy whom George Russell and Katie Tynan had known had been left far behind. So had the successful invader of London drawing-rooms, and the plump individual at whom I had gaped with such curiosity in Abbey Street. He had re-established for the third time his contact with his native country. He was entering his last phase, that period when, white-haired and extremely distinguished-looking, he could look back with satisfaction across more than forty years of sustained and successful effort. Many other men would

* Mrs W. B. Yeats.

43

have felt that the significant part of their life lay behind them. He did not; and if we accept Donald Davie's verdict, the finest portion of his work was still to come. He would publish *The Tower* in 1928, *The Winding Stair and Other Poems* in 1933, and even then there would be nearly as much again to follow, all of it charged with an intense intellectual excitement, none of it ever the mere reiterated afterthoughts of an old man.

I made my way to Merrion Square one Monday evening about half-past eight. I was the first of his guests to arrive. I had come in some trepidation, and trepidation was the last thing to win the poet's approval. However I was young, and he did his best to put me at ease. The young are at a disadvantage on such occasions. If they talk too much, they are liable to be thought egotistical and self-assertive. If they do not talk, they are written off as dull. Before the evening was over I had qualified for condemnation on both counts.

Yeats was a striking figure. The loose silk bow tie—which Rothenstein says was an affectation derived from the French artists and writers of the period—had long since disappeared, and the poet dressed like an aristocrat or country gentleman of breeding. He wore a light-coloured suit of some softly woven tweed material; it was loosely cut and showed to advantage on his tall figure; and the only touches in the least exotic in his appearance were the large silver buckles to his brown leather house-slippers, and the extremely broad black ribbon hanging from the side of his pince-nez. In his poems W. B. often refers to Maud Gonne's eagle look. In fact the epithet is even more appropriate to himself in old age. He had something of the eagle or the hawk in his expression, a proud, interrogatory, searching look, alternating with an oblique, almost sly withdrawal from the perimeter of consciousness, as though he were not actually in a reverie but would like to be thought in one. It was this feeling with Yeats—that even when he

44

appeared to be detached he was really intensely conscious of your presence, assessing you as it were through every tingling pore of his poet's skin—which made contact with him so embarrassing. Even his back spoke volumes.

Possibly it was all a projection of my own excited imagination, and it was my sensitivity to invisible vibrations that was at work and not his; but most people who came in contact with him felt the same.

Yeats never gave the impression of being vain about his poetic achievement. He was far too good a poet, and too serious a poet, to indulge in *hubris*. But he definitely sometimes gave the impression of wishing to overawe and even to humiliate the common-or-garden individual, whose outlook and opinions he despised. Furthermore, it is possible that, being sensitive to atmosphere, he found it trying to be under the eager, adulatory gaze of young disciples, and either played up to them, or else became mannered because of the distress they caused him. It was his defence-mechanism. But after all this has been said, a sediment of real arrogance remained. He disliked and scorned average humanity, the common rut, whose lives seemed to him banal and submissive.

Much of his mannered pose is explained by the fact that he saw life and even the commonest occasion with the pride and intensity of a poet's vision. He magnified everything. I can give a simple illustration of this. Among my papers I find a letter from my mother, in which she passes on a story which Lily Yeats had just told her:

Lily Yeats was telling me that she was lunching at W. B.'s yesterday, and it appears Anne has a little schoolboy friend she is much attached to, and her mother doesn't care much about him and said to her yesterday "I don't know why you are so fond of So-and-so. I don't see anything nice about him," and she replied, "I love his hair, and his eyes are as cold as the coldest March wind." I think she put it more poetically than I am doing. Lily seemed very pleased with it anyway.

So much for the bare outline. Now let us see how Yeats
turns the occasion to his own use. In the series "A Woman
Young and Old" he begins with an eight-line poem, obviously based on this incident, although the rest of the series
has nothing to do with his daughter:

I

FATHER AND CHILD

She hears me strike the board and say
That she is under ban
Of all good men and women,
Being mentioned with a man
That has the worst of all bad names;
And thereupon replies
That his hair is beautiful,
Cold as the March wind his eyes.

The poem is effective enough; but actually I prefer the
stark simplicity of my mother's version.* There one meets
a real occasion and a real child, and Anne's vindication
of her youthful swain rings strikingly true. In the poem
everything has been slightly inflated, and weighed against
the original it brings home sharply to one that Yeatsian
speech is exaggerated speech, just as the Yeatsian manner
could often appear an exaggerated manner.

I was new to the Yeatsian manner that night in Merrion
Square, and certainly it impressed me in the fullest measure.
Yeats was just back from Stockholm, whither he had gone
to receive the Nobel Prize. Lily had already told me that
he had been a great success with the Swedish royal family,
that, alone of the recipients, on that occasion, he seemed to
have some feeling for monarchical ritual and had taken the
trouble to step backwards after receiving his prize from the
royal hands. In his lecture a day or two later he chose
words of singular modesty, saying that an old woman and

* Hone, who must have had the story from Lily, bears out the wording
given by my mother.

46

a young man's ghost ought to have stood on either side of him when he received the prize, and that "when Lady Gregory's name and John Synge's name are spoken by future generations, my name, if remembered, will come up in the talk, and that if my name is spoken first their names will come in their turn because of the years we worked together."

Yeats was full of the architectural beauties of Stockholm. He showed me a book of photographs that he had brought home and expatiated at some length on the dignity and fine proportions of the Town Hall. Presently A. E. arrived and, a little later, Lennox Robinson. These, according to my journal, were the only other visitors that night. A. E. lowered himself into the depth of a big armchair and lit his pipe. Mrs Yeats, so far as I remember, slipped away, leaving us to our talk. I was impressed by the beauty of the high-ceilinged room. It was at the back of the house, overlooking a narrow strip of town garden, with the inevitable Victorian stable at the far end, but was joined by an open double doorway to the front room overlooking Merrion Square. Yeats's books, a few ornaments—Chinese, I rather think—a design by Sturge Moore, a water-colour by Dulac and the magnificent portrait which John Butler Yeats had painted of his brother-in-law George Pollexfen, are what linger in my recollection.

So does the memory of my own ineptitude. At Rathgar Avenue one never went away with the feeling that one had talked too much, for everyone there talked too much. Individuals, little groups of four or five gathered with heads together in the corner, A. E. himself wreathed in smoke in his battered armchair, all poured forth a steady non-stop stream of verbiage. Gentle Mrs Russell was the only person on these occasions who, when she talked, gave the impression that she might have preferred to remain silent.

But tonight at Merrion Square I was a young man in the presence of two of Ireland's greatest talkers, and it would probably have been wiser to have concentrated on the role of listener. It was interesting to watch W. B.'s and A. E.'s technique on these occasions. Both of them loved talking. Both of them, in the phrase of rugby football, hung onto the ball as long as they could, developing their theme closely and continuously, so that a knife-blade could not be thrust between their sentences. But, sooner or later, it was necessary to pause, if only to breathe; and then the other would cut in, instantly, and take up the threnody.

I listened with due reverence; and the talk was intensely interesting. It was as though both great men fully realised that a chiel was among them takin' notes. But at the same time the chiel showed a lamentable propensity, not actually to interrupt, but to do his own share of the talking whenever he got the chance.

Anatole France was mentioned and I repeated the rather curious verdict of W. J. Locke—where I had come across it I cannot imagine—that France was one of the few writers in whom philosophy and poetry had met and the philosopher had not killed the poet. It strikes me as complete nonsense now, if only for the reason that France, although he wrote poetry in youth, carried hardly anything whatever of the poet into maturity. But it irritated Yeats for a different reason.

"Pooh, he has no philosophy at all."

My record of the occasion comments promptly: "Perhaps he is thinking of his own monumental work on the subject which is to be published after his death and which both Fagan and A. S. Owen, with whom he has discussed it, tell me will damage his reputation irretrievably—at any rate he has no patience with the rationalist, any more than A. E. has, preferring his own hotch-potch of symbolism and magic." Obviously I did not like having Anatole France attacked, and my journal continues, rather tartly, "The greatest man is the mystic—Plato, Plotinus, Laotze—but the next greatest is the rationalist, coming like a clear wind

48

to blow away the rubbish that has collected around the other's teaching, thanks to too zealous and altogether blind disciples, and it annoys me to hear Yeats dismiss France so summarily, for he represents, if nothing else, one aspect of the human mind—that of gentle scepticism—almost to perfection. France may be remembered when Yeats is forgotten, or for that matter neither of them may be remembered, but at any rate Yeats with his four symbolic or magic watch-dogs around the four posts of his bed (I have forgotten the poem)* is a less worthy figure than France with his gently expressed doubt."

All this indicates a certain psychological resistance to the man I was meeting for the first time. I plunged into defence of the Frenchman with ardour.

Yeats: "His best book is the *Pédauque* book—what is it called?—the one with the salamanders in it."

A little later he says that he has read the first half of *Penguin Island* with pleasure, but that the second had only infuriated him.

Here at any rate we agree.

"Exactly. The first half is the more philosophic. It is universal satire, satire on human nature. The second half is satire on French history and politics."

The talk passes to Maeterlinck. He secures almost as little approval and after a time I say: "Then you'd place him rather low in the list of Nobel Prize winners?"

There is a sudden explosion of suppressed laughter from the silent Lennox Robinson, who, earlier in the evening, had folded up his angularities like a candle-snuffer into a chair on the far side of the room. It almost dislodges his pince-nez from his nose. I know he is not trying to hurt my feelings. Lennox is a gentle whimsical creature, who might give you a scratch if he thought you deserved it, but

* There is no such poem. I was obviously thinking of a passage in *The Trembling of the Veil* (p. 149) where Yeats says. "In order to keep myself from nightmare, I had formed the habit of imagining four watch-dogs, one at each corner of my room."

who would not go out of his way to hurt anyone's feelings. But his splutter of laughter makes me feel that I have committed a gaffe, and I curse myself for being so ingenuous.

About eleven o'clock we said good night and I walked up with A. E. and Robinson to Harcourt Street Station, where A. E. got his Terenure tram and Robinson and I took the train, I to Dundrum, and he on to Foxrock, where he was living in Sir Horace Plunkett's gate-lodge.

VI

I HAD met the poet at last, the mind that had cast a greater spell of words over my consciousness in youth than almost any other. I had been warned in various ways, by the mocking stories of George Moore in *Hail and Farewell*, and by phrases let drop by Katharine Tynan and her daughter Pamela, not to expect too much. The gentle boy that they had known had been left fár behind. He had outgrown his earlier friends and was capable of snubbing a lord because he happened to be talking to a duke, and so on. But it is doubtful if any of these weighed much with me. What my journal does reveal is a certain instinctive shrinking from his personality. This emerges clearly enough in my attempts to assess him:

Yeats's silver-buckled shoes, his somewhat distrait manner, the perfect taste of the room, suggest not merely the poet and playwright but the senator and politician as well. Yeats's garret days are far behind ... A very great man as anyone can see who reads his reveries over childhood and youth and sees the astonishing sense of the dignity of his calling that he brought to life from the beginning—encouraged by his father—indifferent to everything except the perfection of his art. But his manner, when it is not distrait, is arrogant and unsympathetic and, looking at both men tonight, I think "A. E. is the more likely to go to heaven," for Yeats, although he is the greater artist and perhaps the greater intellect, has none of A. E.'s sympathy and benevolence, and there is something of the crank and magician about him, whereas there is nothing about A. E. that is not wholesome and human. A. E. will talk to Plato and to Socrates in the Elysian Fields, but Yeats will be among the black magic folk, and I think to myself "A. E. is the truer mystic

51

of the two." Yeats will not look you in the face, at least not until he has been talking to you for some time. There is something cold about him, something inhuman; he is more like a hawk than the rook of George Moore's reminiscence. Perhaps it is the great hooked nose and the hard expression of the wide mouth. I am overawed by the man whose work I admire so intensely, but not into silence. Nervousness perhaps makes me talk more, or anxiety to vindicate my being there at all. At any rate I talk an inordinate amount on every subject that comes up and create, I begin to feel, an extremely bad impression.

Russell had won me to his side immediately by his radiating benevolence. W. B. repelled me by his sensitive hauteur. The contrast between the two friends was so great that it aroused a conflict of loyalties straight away. Yeats was fully aware of this. His sneers against A. E.'s literary disciples, his quarrels with Dunsany, Seumas O'Sullivan and Austin Clarke, his break with George Moore, are all subtly linked with the devotion which these men showed to his boyhood companion. I myself found that I could never sit in a room with W. B. and A. E. without my homage going out instinctively to the one, and without weighing continually and almost instinctively A. E.'s essential goodness against all the curious twists and semi-occult turns in the great poet's character.

And yet they were both committed to the occult, someone may say. Yes, but in an entirely different fashion. A. E. had taken the path of Bhakti Yoga, redemption by the practice of self-discipline and good works; W. B. had followed all sorts of curious by-paths and side-turnings, spiritualism, Rosicrucianism and so on. Their ways had diverged from the moment when Yeats first went to London, and in 1900 we find Russell writing to his friend: "In mysticism and in our ideas we have little or nothing in common . . . if I held your ideas I would never write another line."

My first visit had not been a success, but my second,

about five weeks later, went off much better. This time my journal tells me that I went determined to enforce silence on myself. Yeats was alone when I arrived, and for a time we discussed the subject of rhythm in prose and verse. I reminded him of Lynd's saying that the English language had not possessed certain rhythms until he introduced them, and this pleased him. A. E. arrived and Lyle Donaghy and the talk turned on Christianity. Yeats appeared to be arguing against the idea of a historical Jesus, and yet professed himself amazed by the truth of the whole story, viewed in a symbolic light and in relation to similar myths. A. E. trotted out his stock criticism of Christianity: "No cosmogony, no psychology, only a most perfect ethic." It is a criticism not wholly true, for the psychology of many of the parables and sayings in the Gospels is profound, the house swept and garnished for seven devils to enter being one example. They then began to debate whether the Jesus of the Gospels had ever existed, or whether the real Jesus was not a certain obscure Yesu, who had lived exactly a hundred years before. I have found the same contention in various modern rehashes of occult doctrine. It was a favourite gambit in post-Blavatsky circles. But this was the first time I had ever heard it, and I pricked up my ears like a hare, suddenly alert amid alien corn. From there they went on to discuss certain mental visions which they had had in youth. A. E. described one which he believed was of St John the Divine. He had followed a youth through many streets, and later found himself in a low cave where a figure in the centre was being massaged by those around him. Initiation was mentioned. Various initiations were discussed, and then I think W. B. remarked, "Of course death is the great moment of initiation for every man."

I listened in wonder to all this, drinking it in, if not open-mouthed, at least with every sign of respectful interest. This was better behaviour on my part than counter-attacks

53

on behalf of Anatole France. And it created a considerably better impression. Drinks were produced, tea for A. E., whisky, a bottle of white wine. Madame Blavatsky was mentioned and they began to discuss her credentials. Donaghy reminded them that the Society for Psychical Research had come down heavily against her. Lennox Robinson mentioned the occasion when there had been one cup short at a picnic with the Sinnetts. Madame Blavatsky had pointed to a certain spot on the hillside and told them to dig, and lo—a china cup, matching the rest of the set, clean and recently materialised, which completely solved their dilemma.

"The ground was undisturbed where they dug?"

"Yes, but it was pointed out later that the hill was steep and that, by digging a little shaft straight down from the roots of the tree, the cup could have been buried, and then rediscovered by digging into the hillside from a different angle."

A. E. sat silent through all this, placidly puffing his pipe. He did not take up cudgels for Blavatsky, nor can I remember Yeats doing so either. Lennox and the Society for Psychical Research were left in possession of the field.

It had been a more interesting evening than the previous one and I had enjoyed it. It had delighted me to hear them describing and discussing visionary experiences, and I had been too interested to want to talk, beyond saying:

"You know you are like men returning from a country I know nothing of."

"Quite so," said Yeats, "and it is right that you should remind us of it." And coming down to the hall with us he said good night in a more kindly fashion, remembering my name which he had certainly not done when I arrived.

I walked up to Harcourt Street with A. E. Now was the moment to question him about his visions.

"I don't understand. Do you really see these things? I mean do you see them subjectively or objectively?"

"I don't know what you mean by subjective or objective," he replied rather angrily. "I really see them. And another witness at the same time has corroborated what I have reported, correcting me in this detail or on that." Then he added solemnly: "I am convinced that there is another world about this world, more beautiful in every way and possessed by men and women far above us." It was as if this great bearded figure, lumbering slowly along beside me, were offering me his first-hand witness of the heaven-world that Plato described. He had seen into it in the same way that Israel's leader had gazed down on the sunlit promised land. And he spoke of it as a real world, verifiable in terms of experience. *In Hail and Farewell* when Moore questions him about the three god-like figures who had appeared at his bedside, A. E. will not say whether he saw them "as one sees something reflected in a mirror or as I am seeing you now." But to me he seemed to be asserting direct vision into a world lying about and interpenetrating ours, a coloured, happy world in which sorrow had no part.

He began to tell me of his seven years of mystic culture with his friends in the house in Ely Place. He might have gone further, much further in the path of attainment, but he had had to give it up—the practice of intense mental concentration and all the rest—because it was beginning to tell on his health.

Then, as though reproaching himself for not having gone to her defence earlier in the evening, he said defiantly:

"They may say what they like about Blavatsky, but I have seen her do some wonderful things."

I have discussed elsewhere this question of A. E.'s possible personal contact with the foundress of Theosophy. There is no record of it; he possessed a signed photograph of her, and became a member of her Esoteric Section a few months before her death; but, apart from a single allusion by Pryse many years later, after A. E.'s death, to having

55

first met him at Theosophical headquarters in London, and this remark to me, I know no evidence at all of his having been outside Ireland in early manhood. Nevertheless it seems highly likely, and his great friend Harry Norman supported the contention.

At Harcourt Street we were still talking about Madame and he was recommending me to read *The Secret Doctrine*. "It is the only one of her books that really matters. There you will find it all."

More than thirty years have gone by and I have still to obey his injunction and get hold of the book. Ordinarily, if consulted upon "the path," A. E. would recommend the *Bhagavad-gita* and *Patanjali*. But if you asked him about Blavatsky it was always *The Secret Doctrine*. Once when I asked him what of importance had been written on the subject of reincarnation his reply was "McTaggart. McTaggart is the only modern writer who has said anything to the point." McTaggart was duly sought out in the National Library, but I did not find him very stimulating.

VII

I HAD spent two evenings in the poet's company, nevertheless I felt further from him rather than nearer to him as a result. L. A. G. Strong, who knew him as well as any of the younger generation did, and who was devoted to him, says:

Yeats was a difficult man to know, not because he was aloof . . . but because he had so many sides and lived on such a high plane of intelligence. He was reserved about his personal life, though he spoke freely of his ideas, and those who had spent hours with him would realise afterwards that, while they had been encouraged to speak of their concerns, Yeats had said nothing about his. So Yeats's *Autobiographies* tell a great deal about his mind, but are incomplete on the emotional side. "Being in love, and in no way lucky in that love:" that is his only account of an experience that provided the finest love poetry in modern English, and, for the very reason that Yeats so ruthlessly made his life serve his art, we cannot read back from the poems to the man. Thus we are unlikely to know more than he tells us. Those who are interested to investigate what use the poet made of his emotions, and therefore wish to gauge the intensity of the emotions in the man, will find that he has covered his tracks with an old fox's cunning.

That is well stated, but in my own experience it was not quite as simple as that. I agree with the main contention that Yeats hid his essential nature from the curious eyes of the world. There are several possible reasons for this. In youth and early manhood he had devoted himself to building up and deliberately buttressing his poetic personality. He wished to be the poet and he wished to look the poet.

57

Ernest Boyd has said: "Yeats is the only writer in our time who not only did not look ridiculous in flowing tie, long hair and jacket of sombre black or even velvet, but looked more properly attired than in the conventional garments of later years." This emphasis upon his vocation had brought a certain amount of scorn upon him in his early days. At a time when I was writing a thesis on the youth of A. E., I ran to earth in the *Dublin Evening Telegraph* for 14 January 1888 a most caustic article entitled "A Dublin Literary Coterie Sketched by a Non-Pretentious Observer." It is unsigned, but from a feminine hand, beginning, "A young lady moving in Dublin society sends us the following sketch from social life in this city." In it Katharine Tynan, Yeats and George Russell (who refers to the article in a letter to his friend Carrie Rea) are all cruelly lampooned. Katharine Tynan is Sappho. Russell is O'Reilly, "an artist, allegorical and mystic, so very earnest and so preternaturally clever as to be enveloped in pretty pathos." Yeats is Augustus Fitzgibbon, and the anonymous lady critic is hardest of all upon him:

Augustus Fitzgibbon, considered by himself and his friends to be a poet of titanic power, who may accomplish great things and who may not, but whose boyish head is being in the meantime turned in the most delightful and most deplorable fashion by the circle which is fortunate enough to revolve round this elsewhere unappreciated star. His friends will gravely tell you that Ireland has produced no such poet hitherto; that some of his unpublished songs are equal to Shakespeare, that in music he ranks with Shelley, in colouring with Keats, and that Coleridge himself was not more saturated with deep and transcendental philosophy. They will tell you that he is too exquisite and ethereal to be understood or appreciated by the common British reviewer and hence his obscurity. All this of course Fitzgibbon fondly believes, and invites you to believe by the ingratiating sweetness with which he takes his spoiling. In his circle all are equally sincere in giving and returning flattery.

Both in his own home and amongst his friends Yeats had

complete acceptance, his genius was recognised and he was regarded as a being apart. Later he plunged into the rough and tumble of journalism, and of theatrical enterprise. But, long before that, he had built a high palisade around his personality to protect it from the intrusive gaze of the world. And, linked with this need of personal privacy, which Strong notes, was his theory of style. The subject became an obsession with him. Originally style meant an escape from the flat banalities of conventional poetic diction to a more natural and living speech freed from affectation. But in fact what Yeats eventually did was to reject the windy bourgeois eloquence of patriotic verse and replace it by another and different eloquence which was aristocratic and purely personal. Style became an end in itself; a poet's first duty was to speak with individual distinction.

It was this ceaseless self-cultivation according to plan, this building up of the poetic personality for a deliberate purpose, that may in the end have helped to make Yeats seem a little unreal. A. E. had disciplined and shaped himself in youth just as severely but with an altogether different aim. His objective was that of every religious mystic, first moral goodness, and then, as one of the results, insight and wisdom. What Yeats wanted was golden-tongued speech for its own sake. Or rather he wanted that most of all. In fact he had a vigorous and questing intellect, credulous in some respects, sceptical in others. But his reaction to any accepted school of religious or philosophic thought was instinctively that of the rebel. He had as great a contempt for the modes of thought of the herd as for their modes of speech; and, though he could be heard periodically regretting his "lack of education," his metaphysical arrogance is almost as great as that of Madame Blavatsky. Yeats's attitude to religion was not unlike that of an old maid who has been crossed in love in her youth and finds it hard to forget. He reveals the fact for an instant when in *Autobiographies* he writes of what he calls the Tragic Generation:

59

Why are these strange souls born everywhere to-day, with hearts that Christianity, as shaped by history, cannot satisfy? ... Why should we believe that religion can never bring round its antithesis? Is it true that our air is disturbed, as Mallarmé said, by "the trembling of the veil of the Temple," or that "our whole age is seeking to bring forth a sacred book"? Some of us thought that book near towards the end of last century, but the tide sank again.

For a flash—in that last sentence—he lifts the curtain on what perhaps had been one of the hopes of his youth. He and his Theosophic and Rosicrucian friends had imagined themselves on the threshold of a new revelation. But it had all come to nothing; what had begun in grandiloquent dreams of power had ended for men like his friend MacGregor Mathers in melancholy or suicide. A. E. had abandoned membership of the Theosophical Society but he had remained a Theosophist, in that he continued to seek truth in the different great religions of the world. Because he was, in large measure, the product of the moral earnestness of a Christian home, and because he was fundamentally religious, he had evolved a religion of his own, which even his opponents had to respect. It came back really to three tenets, a belief in goodness and the possibility of self-improvement, a firm belief in man's spiritual nature, and a belief that we live many earthly lives and not merely one. A. E.'s, as the *Church Times* wrote after his death, "was a soul that was naturally Christian." Yeats, although he might have his children baptised, was an anti-cleric, scornful of the organised Churches, and instinctively opposed to their paternalism. He was not interested in their moral and ethical teaching as such; he shared all his father's contempt for the tame submission to authority of the unthinking masses; and he had nothing of the mystic's thirst for self-perfection. What he and his friends in youth had hoped to do was to overthrow materialism and storm the kingdom of heaven in a frontal attack by the discovery of latent powers in themselves. I am not sure what he intended by that sentence, "Why should we believe that religion can never bring round its antithesis?" It is one of those *obiter dicta* which fell from time to time from his lips and which you were not expected to question. Perhaps it means that organised religion can end by producing the very opposite of its avowed intention, which is spirituality; and certain epochs in church history almost seem to favour the hypothesis. But in *The Trembling of the Veil* we meet nothing that suggests spiritual recrudescence; Mathers and his friends are not mystics, they are occultists and magic-mongers, filled with a pathetic sense of their own importance, which, as Yeats points out, was partly compensation for a sense of insecurity.

Nothing was to come of it all; and when he writes of these people in his autobiography, Yeats does so humorously, or else with devastating, although perhaps unintentional, irony. He moved at this time in a circle of eccentrics and oddities, and his own mood seems to have alternated between faith and despair. On one page we read, "In the credulity of our youth we secretly wondered if he [MacGregor Mathers] had not met with, perhaps even been taught by, some old man who had found the elixir. Nor did he undeceive us:" on the next, "A conviction that the world was now but a bundle of fragments possessed me without ceasing." In considering the later man all this is highly relevant. Yeats was not a scholar, not a mystic, not a metaphysician. He was a most gifted poet, who in youth had dabbled in the occult, had glued his eye to the keyhole, and had brought back disjointed rumours of the mystery which lay beyond. In attempting to establish the autonomy of the mind and the importance of image and symbol, his motive may have been "religious" in the sense that it was a counter-attack on the arrogance of the dialectical materialists: but the hallmark of the occultist is his belief in his own powers, whereas the hallmark of the mystic is

61

his surrender to Tao, to God, to the Power which lies outside himself. It is astonishing how entirely self-willed all
Yeats's intellectual processes were. He despised the traditional and the accepted, on principle.

> Grant me an old man's frenzy,
> Myself must I remake
> Till I am Timon and Lear
> Or that William Blake
> Who beat upon the wall
> Till Truth obeyed his call.

It is significant that he does not pray to be remade, but to
remake. His Russian prophetess had committed him to this
defiant individualism. But what real sage would ever wish
to be either Lear or Timon of Athens? His angry dualism,
his disappointed Messianic hopes, reveal themselves in
lines like:

> I mock Plotinus' thought
> And cry in Plato's teeth.

Plato is the supreme poet-philosopher. Plotinus is the
supreme philosopher-mystic. Beside their patient, closely-
reasoned views, steeped in philosophic and moral conviction, Yeats's speculations and guesses at truth are mere psychological flotsam. But because these names are accepted
and honoured they arouse the rebel in the poet, and in
this he seems to be the forerunner of a whole generation.

VIII

IN Yeats's nature were the seeds of many possible conflicts.
There was the philosophic conflict, a conflict between a
man in search of a system and one who could cry, "he is a
logician and a logician is a fool when life, which is a thing
of emotion, is in question." There was the religious conflict,
between a Yeats who could pray and who had had his
children baptised and one with a Luciferian complex and a
dislike of all "the black-coated gentlemen," and whose
mysticism A. E. realised had practically nothing in common
with his own. And lastly there was the conflict in the blood,
the conflict which exists for so many of us, between the
lover as idealist and romanticist, and the lover in carnal
need.

It was this last conflict which perhaps comes nearest
to explaining the man. We can learn a lot from his love
poems, and then from those poems of his old age where the
theme is not love but copulation. "His last play," writes
Strong, "is a riot of copulation and other men's jokes, lit
by flashes of tremendous and erratic poetry." Since the
sexual problem in every individual differs with the strength
of instinct and the code of conduct imposed by self or by
circumstance, it is folly ever to generalise. But in Yeats
one thing is crystal-clear. As a young man he drew the
inspiration for some of his finest poetry from the love which
Maud Gonne inspired but did not return. The force of this
passion was lifelong, where his muse was concerned. As
well, we know of one love affair with a married woman,
which probably lasted for a number of years, and then of

his marriage at the age of fifty-two. Even had he wished to do so, it would have been difficult for him to marry sooner, unless he had married a fortune. Lily Yeats once told me that until quite late in life his total earnings from his books brought him in less than two hundred pounds a year. As well therefore as the "barren passion" he had this motive for remaining single. Finally in old age Yeats, who, it should be made clear, did not suggest the libertine, becomes preoccupied with bodily love, returns again and again to the theme, and even avows defiantly:

> You think it horrible that lust and rage
> Should dance attention upon my old age;
> They were not such a plague when I was young;
> What else have I to spur me into song?

Strong speaks of his covering up his tracks with the cunning of an old fox, but in fact Yeats has been extraordinarily frank about his attitude to women. It is perfectly easy to match the picture which Katharine Tynan draws of him in youth with the existence of a highly idealised but consuming love. Nor, if we know human nature, is there anything irreconcilably contradictory between youth's desire to spread the heaven's embroidered cloths beneath the feet of the beloved and the later note of harsh and crude sexuality. The latter may have been in some measure a reaction against the former. Or, from the moment when he abandoned hope of ever being loved by Maud Gonne, and accepted consolation elsewhere, Yeats, like many another man, may have felt in some measure the renegade of love, unable now ever to reconcile fully spirit and sense, because destiny seemed to have decreed that they should follow different paths.

In *Hail and Farewell* Moore reports at some length a discussion amongst some of his Dublin friends as to whether Yeats's love poetry was written out of a fulfilled or an unfulfilled passion. To him the question seemed crucial. To John Eglinton it was an irrelevance.

A. E. defends his friend: "The love we are considering has lasted for many years and will continue, and I know for certain that it has always been a pure love;" a remark which infuriates Moore, who cries, "A detestable phrase, A. E.! for it implies that every gratified love must be impure."

"Love that has not been born again in the flesh crumbles like peat ash," was Moore's final word. But the evidence points to its crumbling into some remarkably fine poetry. Dante's love for Beatrice, Petrarch's for Laura, are examples of "ungratified passion." Ronsard did not write better poetry about Marie, who had been his mistress, and who died when she was twenty-one, than in *Les Amours d'Hélène* which were inspired by what Brereton calls "the disciplined love of a man of fifty for a young woman of high breeding from whom he scarcely expects more than friendship." Moore's strongest argument that *Tristan and Isolde* owed everything to the surrender of Mathilde Wesendonck, whose calm and lovely face confronts one in white marble in the Villa Wesendonck in Zürich, has been taken from him by the recent publication of the letter which had caused Minna Wagner so much jealousy. It turns out to be very far from the incriminating document that her fevered fancy had made it.

Yeats's love for Maud Gonne sundered his personality to some extent. Henceforward there would always be a cleavage between love as an ideal and love as an instinct. André Maurois has spoken of the "incalculable forces which have been generated by romantic love. Directly or indirectly it has inspired our finest works of art, our greatest works of action." But he also says: "The true romance form of love is always the source of tragedies, because the lovers who have enjoyed for a moment the sense of possessing something perfect and superhuman, long to make that moment eternal. But it is the nature of all things human to be fleeting."

What is so amazing is the hold exercised over Yeats's imagination for years to come by this one great passion. He draws inspiration from it again and again. Other poets, looking back on love, have their sentimental moments, of little real significance; but with Yeats it is not a question of stirring the dead embers; he is always able to make us feel the living flame. He has only to remember what love once meant to him to speak in a different tone. There is nothing harsh or angry about this, only complete authenticity:

> Speech after long silence; it is right,
> All other lovers being estranged or dead,
> Unfriendly lamplight hid under its shade,
> The curtains drawn upon unfriendly night,
> That we descant and yet again descant
> Upon the supreme theme of Art and Song:
> Bodily decrepitude is wisdom; young
> We loved each other and were ignorant.

He admired women. He could say the most lovely and astonishing things about them, like:

> The innocent and the beautiful
> Have no enemy but time.

But it was the memory of one woman and one experience in youth which remained with him longest and could furnish him with inspiration to the end of his days. Other women were nothing by comparison.

If head and limb have beauty and the instep's high and light
They can spread out what sail they please for all I have to say,
Be but the breakers of men's hearts or engines of delight:
I knew a phoenix in my youth, so let them have their day.

He could praise her, twelve years after he had first seen her:

> I thought of your beauty, and this arrow,
> Made out of a wild thought, is in my marrow.
> There's no man may look upon her, no man,
> As when newly grown to be a woman,

66

Tall and noble but with face and bosom
Delicate in colour as apple blossom.
This beauty's kinder, yet for a reason
I could weep that the old is out of season.

He might reproach:

Never give all the heart, for love
Will hardly seem worth thinking of
To passionate women if it seem
Certain, and they never dream
That it fades out from kiss to kiss . . .

Or even denigrate:

Have I not seen the loveliest woman born
Out of the mouth of Plenty's horn,
Because of her opinionated mind
Barter that horn and every good
By quiet natures understood
For an old bellows full of angry wind?

But he could never forget:

And what of her that took
All till my youth was gone
With scarce a pitying look?
How could I praise that one?
When day begins to break
I count my good and bad,
Being wakeful for her sake,
Remembering what she had,
What eagle look still shows,
While up from my heart's root
So great a sweetness flows
I shake from head to foot.

No one could write like that years afterwards unless he
had loved indeed.

In fact it is almost certain that idealised love and sensual
love had both figured in Yeats's poetry at the time when
Moore asked his question. When Hone was working on his
biography, I remember his telling me that a number of

67

Yeats's love poems were written to Mrs Shakespear. And in his book he specifically allots her the delightful:

> One had a lovely face,
> And two or three had charm,
> But charm and face were in vain
> Because the mountain grass
> Cannot but keep the form
> Where the mountain hare has lain.

She was a young London hostess when Yeats first met her, married to an elderly solicitor whom the poet saw but once. After Olivia Shakespear's death Yeats wrote to a friend: "For more than forty years she has been the centre of my life in London, and during all that time we have never had a quarrel, sadness sometimes but never a difference. When I first met her she was in her late twenties but in looks a lovely young girl. When she died she was a lovely old woman."

She was indeed a beautiful woman, by all accounts; and it is probable that she took possession of Yeats, more gently but in something the same fashion that Shaw's stormy *inamorata* did of him about the same time. One can see from Yeats's letters to her that she was a good and loyal friend. But I find myself conceding to her only those of the love poems which I like least. She can have—what was probably hers—all the stagey and highfalutin stuff about curlews crying in the wind, passion-dimmed eyes and long heavy hair shaken out over the breast. She was possibly in his mind when he wrote:

> I bring you with reverent hands
> The book of my numberless dreams,
> White woman that passion has worn
> As the tide wears the dove-grey sands.

It was her beauty probably which was "kinder" in the poem already quoted, but which left him weeping for the old which was out of season. And it is she and Maud Gonne

who are, almost certainly, together in his mind, at some
early stage of the later friendship, when he writes:

The Lover Mourns for the Loss of Love

Pale brows, still hands and dim hair,
I had a beautiful friend
And dreamed that the old despair
Would end in love in the end:
She looked in my heart one day
And saw your image was there;
She has gone weeping away.

The mere shadow of the phoenix had been sufficient
instantly to frighten away her rival. He may have owed
much to the friendship of Olivia Shakespear, but the most
original and the most moving of the love poetry is Maud
Gonne's. There are those who contend that a man loves
deeply only once in his life, and there is plenty of ammuni-
tion for their argument scattered through Yeats's poems.
He reverts again and again to this early love.

Whereon I wrote and wrought,
And now, being grey,
I dream that I have brought
To such a pitch my thought
That coming time can say,
"He shadowed in a glass
What thing her body was."

For she had fiery blood
When I was young,
And trod so sweetly proud
As 'twere upon a cloud,
A woman Homer sung,
That life and letters seem
But an heroic dream.

Repeatedly he stresses that his love for her was real, but
that her rejection of it had made him transmute it into
mere words. Great as his loyalty was to his vocation, he can

69

regret that she forced him towards it rather than towards life:

> That every year I have cried, "At length
> My darling understands it all,
> Because I have come into my strength,
> And words obey my call;"

> That had she done so who can say
> What would have shaken from the sieve?
> I might have thrown poor words away
> And been content to live.

All this rings truer than the slightly cloying sentiment of the poems which I suspect were written to Mrs Shakespear and which strike a note of nostalgia and vague melancholy rather in the manner of Keats's:

> A heart high sorrowful and cloyed,
> A burning forehead, and a parching tongue.

Here Yeats can write lines which are sickly and almost *fin de siècle*:

> Your eyes that once were never weary of mine
> Are bowed in sorrow under pendulous lids,
> Because our love is waning.

That clearly is not concerned with Maud Gonne. There follows a reference, thrown in, one suspects, to placate the lady, to

> that hour of gentleness
> When the poor tired child, Passion, falls asleep.

And, finally, with

> How far away the stars seem, and how far
> Is our first kiss, and ah, how old my heart!

we feel quite sure that the whole thing is just another Japanese fan and bamboo furniture affair of the 1890's. The poem ends with Yeats thinking about a succession of

70

reincarnations, not, one should perhaps point out today, a succession of week-ends:

> "Ah, do not mourn," he said,
> "That we are tired, for other loves await us;
> Hate on and love through unrepining hours.
> Before us lies eternity; our souls
> Are love, and a continual farewell."

If this is the poetry of a realised passion, how much better is that of the unrealised. He cannot speak of Maud Gonne without evoking her effect upon him and the background of their two lives. She had always commanded the affection and devotion of the simple and humble, and he remembers this in the midst of social contacts which bore and distress him:

> She is foremost of those that I would hear praised.
> I have gone about the house, gone up and down
> As a man does who has published a new book,*
> Or a young girl dressed out in her new gown,
> And though I have turned the talk by hook or crook
> Until her praise should be the uppermost theme,
> A woman spoke of some new tale she had read,
> A man confusedly in a half dream
> As though some other name ran in his head.

> She is foremost of those that I would hear praised.
> I will talk no more of books or the long war
> But walk by the dry thorn until I have found
> Some beggar sheltering from the wind, and there
> Manage the talk until her name come round.
> If there be rags enough he will know her name
> And be well pleased remembering it, for in the old days,
> Though she had young men's praise and old men's blame,
> Among the poor both old and young gave her praise.

This is from the heart and is worth pages of nonsense about the poor tired child Passion. When Van Wyck

---

* Lily Yeats once told me how W. B. was inseparable from his first volume, going everywhere with it tucked firmly under his arm.

Brooks came to Dublin about 1951 he asked me to take him
to see Maud Gonne. I said that I was prejudiced against
her; that she seemed to me a firebrand, committed always
to opposition; a fanatic who, when she and Mrs Despard
settled in my father's parish about the time of the Black
and Tans and he called upon them, met him on the doorstep
and explained to him that, if he came in, he must speak
either French or Irish because they refused to sully their
lips with the English language at that moment. To the end
her sympathies were instinctively with all malcontents.

Nevertheless I rang her daughter-in-law and arranged the
visit. Maud Gonne was in her eighties at this time. It must
have been within a year or so of her death. The last time I
had seen her—tall, gaunt, ashen-pale, her face graven with
a thousand wrinkles—she was in her widow's weeds in the
aisle of the Gaiety Theatre at a matinée given to support
the memorial fund after the death of the poet F. R. Higgins.
Now, her daughter-in-law explained to me, she no longer
went out, but stayed in bed all day and sometimes got up
in the evening about eight o'clock to receive visitors.

I and my wife dined with Brooks and his at the Shelbourne, and we then took the bus out to Clonskeagh. It
brought us to the avenue gate. Maud Gonne was already
downstairs, sunk in a huge deep armchair by the wood fire,
awaiting us. The broad-browed face was more deeply lined
than any face that I have ever seen. Her long, thin, heavily
veined hands rested upon her lap. She was a tall, frail old
lady, but her magnetism was as great as ever. She cast a
spell over me that night, though it was the last thing that
I had expected. I had seen a great life-size photograph of
her as a young woman, lent some years before to a photo-
graphic exhibition at the Mansion House. But in it her good
looks had seemed to me almost too typical. She was the
tall, Junoesque, full-bosomed beauty of the time, almost the
Gibson girl. Here was nothing unique or special, but simply
a fine, handsome young woman such as every Edwardian

72

MAUD GONNE IN OLD AGE

drawing-room delighted in, a mere social beauty, not that radiant creature whom Hone describes as playing with a spray of flowers by the window of John Butler Yeats's house in Blenheim Road when W. B. first saw her.

The photograph had left me unmoved. But she was to subdue me completely now in her old age. I think what won my heart finally was when Mrs Van Wyck Brooks asked her how it came about that she, an English army officer's daughter, should have become the prophetess of Irish nationalism. She thought for a moment and then said, "Well, when I was still quite a little girl I used to go riding through the country on a pony beside my father. It was the time of the evictions and I used to see people standing in front of their unroofed cottages from which the police held them back, and weeping bitterly. I thought to myself, 'When I grow up I'm going to change all that. Yes, I'm going to change all that.' "

As she said it the years vanished and we seemed to be looking into the heart of a little girl of nine who saw herself in imagination as another Joan of Arc, and with a tightening of the lips had decided for herself the whole matter. When *she* grew up such things would be impossible; people would no longer weep outside the homes where they had lived.

I was converted. The spell had been cast over me also. She seemed all grace and charm, an enchantress of men's hearts despite her eighty years, and when we rose to go it was I, her detractor, who raised her heavily-veined brown hand and kissed it.

Destiny, nature, God, his own efforts—all these made Yeats a great poet. But she had clinched the matter. Whenever he mentions her in his verse he speaks on the old note of wonder. She was not to resolve the problems of his life. Rather she was to make them more acute. He would follow "a road of inner confusion," to use her own phrase. But it was she who touched his lips with a coal of fire and helped to make him the singer he was.

73

IX

SOON after my second visit to Yeats, I departed to Prestatyn in North Wales to take up a teaching post in a boys' preparatory school. When A. E. heard that I was going, he instantly remembered that John Eglinton was settled there and gave me an introduction to him. John Eglinton—W. K. Magee, to give him his real name—was already familiar to me from the pages of *Hail and Farewell*. I found him friendly and hospitable. He had been at school at different times with both Yeats and A. E., and he described to me how in his later schooldays W. B., although an indifferent scholar, had been looked upon by the other boys as one apart. He was incompetent to do any ordinary classwork, and indeed hardly troubled at all by the masters, but his prestige with the rest of the school nevertheless stood high. He seemed older in himself than they, and already he had a virgin beard. A. E., John Eglinton maintained, was quiet, shy and extraordinarily diffident, in contrast to his later eloquence; but this picture does not altogether agree with the accounts given to me by his other school-fellows, the Rev. H. Brown and Goodwillie.

I found life as an usher in a small, strictly disciplined school, under a highly plethoric, elderly, clerical headmaster, far from easy. One of its few solaces was John Eglinton. Another was my weekly pilgrimage to W. H. Smith & Sons in the town to collect my copy of the *Irish Statesman*. That journal had got well into its stride by now. Without favouring any clique or any generation, A. E. managed to fill it each week with interesting matter, a very large pro-

74

portion written by himself under various pseudonyms. To the younger generation the *Irish Statesman* was a godsend. It gave us an opportunity to see ourselves in print fairly regularly. A. E. accepted poems from me, an occasional long article (that meant one's name was one of the three on the outside cover) and from time to time I was given a book to review. A poem on the mystery of man's existence —the bird flying across the lighted room—which I had inscribed to A. E. personally, was modestly renamed by him "From Disciple to Master" before it found its way into print. Lolly Yeats wrote to me: "I *did* like your poem in the *Statesman*. 'The Pupil to the Master' was that its title? I sent it away—I am getting some extra copies. I promised to get it for the Morehampton Road Yeatses. Mr Best said he liked it greatly."

This was encouraging. But something much more encouraging happened a few weeks later. Lolly had ended the letter by scribbling across the top of it "W. B. is still in Rome." When she next wrote he had returned:

Last week W. B., just as I was leaving for the train, ran down the stairs and called out "Lolly, Lolly, do you know who Monk Gibbon is, for he has a very fine poem in the *Statesman*?" He was really enthusiastic and ran upstairs again to tell his wife that it was yours—the name "Monk" puzzled him. He said "Why Monk?" I said it was your Christian name. "Very good—very good" then said he. I knew you would be pleased with his approval. He was only just back a few days from Italy and must have been methodically going through the *Statesmen* that had collected in his absence.

Lolly was showing her customary kindness in telling me this and in plenty of other ways. I was proposing to get some of my poems printed as a small book in Guernsey, a project that, like many others, came to nothing. But Lolly was willing to help by doing a drawing for me and making a small block of it for the title-page. She was also anxious

75

to get something from me for the series of cards that her press printed at Christmas:

Have you written any verses on Friendship? I want something to do with Christmas, but not the religious side of Christmas. Nearly all the Christmas verses are religious—and people want the other note as well—about eight lines—meetings of family—festivity—quiet happiness, joy and children—something that would *make a picture* and not long, to have room for an actual picture on the folded sheet.

When I saw her in Ireland she told me that W. B., hearing of her request, had commented, "He is too young to write an 'occasional' poem. It was years before I could even attempt to write a poem to order."

He was probably right, but I duly mixed the ingredients given to me and presently sent off my eight lines, which, with a picture by Beatrice Elvery of the Goddess of Fortune suddenly appearing in an Irish crofter's cottage to pour out largesse from her horn of plenty, met the occasion. At any rate Lolly seemed pleased.

I like greatly "The Windy Hill." I think I won't show it to W. B. till we have printed it. I will see—I don't want him to get the idea he can *edit* our cards as well as our books. I might never have got any verses at all—he does not realise that a Christmas card to sell must have the accepted Christmas spirit. I like your poem greatly and I believe he will too.

History does not relate whether he did or not. But when, a few weeks later, I returned to Ireland at Easter, there ensued one of the most amicable of my contacts with the poet. John Eglinton was the Irish correspondent of the American *Dial*, and while I was in Prestatyn I had frequent opportunities of borrowing its latest number from him. Of all the literary journals of that time Desmond MacCarthy's *Life and Letters* and the *Dial* were by far the best. MacCarthy once complained to me that the young men whose talents he fostered in *Life and Letters* never had a good word to say for the paper and never lifted a finger to save it.

76

The *Dial* failed also when the generous young American, upon whose financial backing it depended, became ill and his subsidies ceased. It was a grave pity because the standard of creative writing and of criticism was extremely high in both papers.

It was in the pages of the *Dial* that I first met the two philosophers Spengler and Keyserling, who were soon to make a considerable stir in the thought of the 1920's. I was as quick to fall for them as anyone. The eclectic in Keyserling appealed to me. I was a good deal of one myself, and I had always admired the way in which A. E. sought not for the divergencies of thought in different systems but for their similarities. Both Keyserling and Spengler were to be the subject of long articles written by me for the *Irish Statesman* when their books appeared in translation. But when I returned to Dublin in April, Keyserling's *The Travel Diary of a Philosopher* had not yet been published in English, and references to him and to Spengler—whose work had been partially translated in the *Dial*—had scarcely begun to appear in English journals.

Soon after getting home—possibly after a visit to A. E. at Plunkett House nearby—I encountered Yeats almost in front of the doorway of 82 Merrion Square and plunged immediately into animated and friendly conversation with him. To live out of Ireland and then to return to the stimulus of Dublin literary life and Dublin conversation always unsealed my lips, not that they ever needed much unsealing. It was wonderful to re-enter the world of ideas and to pour forth one's views with the energy of a stream that has been dammed for weeks and then suddenly liberated. Ordinarily this impetuosity and ebullience would have met with little favour from W. B., but on this occasion, and by a happy accident, it was welcome. Spengler was the topic dominant in my thoughts at the moment, and I no sooner mentioned him and some of his ideas than Yeats became immediately interested. For Spengler with his doctrine of historical sequence, his theory that a society passes through certain inevitable phases, first becoming a "culture," and then a "civilisation," until presently it ceases to be prompted by valid internal forces and becomes the victim of its own technological mastery of the external, was of intense interest to someone who had been working out a semi-mystical system of the different phases through which human personality is taken in the course of a series of incarnations. When men cease to make a single affirmation concerning the universe and to predicate the Ineffable —God, Brahma, Tao—an affirmation which, although it proves nothing, asserts a definite relationship between man's helplessness and the vastness of the mystery which surrounds him, they soon find themselves striving to fill the void created, by words of some sort or other. Some pattern must be evolved; an anthropological pattern; a psychological pattern; an historical pattern. A sage like A. E., descending from his own particular Mount Sinai, is liable to find the intelligentsia grouped in reverent adoration round a new golden calf, such as "the Subconscious." One can almost suggest the ritual of the sect, a rather monotonous chant "Great is the Subconscious and all things must ultimately be referred to it!"

The 1920's were a happy hunting ground for all those who sought disciples for a new generalisation. Lawrence's doctrine of the blood, Freud's libido, then seemed likely to unlock every door. Yeats's theory of the twenty-six phases of human character was too subtle, too esoteric ever to attract a large following, but it was a symptom of the general disposition to turn away from the accepted—the babbled shibboleths of doctrine that has been hardened by general acceptance, and is imposing itself from an authoritarian basis rather than an evangelical one—and to try and find something better in pastures altogether new. The age of pious or hypocritical submission was over. The age of chaotic ferment had begun.

Spengler had a better case than many. Flinders Petrie had already suggested that civilisations followed one another in rhythmic succession, that the wave rises slowly, gathers force, breaks and is dispersed. What excited Yeats was to learn, from my very brief outline of the Spenglerian doctrine, that the German's thought in so many respects ran parallel to his own. He had worked now for a number of years on the automatic scripts which his wife had begun to write down while they were still on their honeymoon. It was not the ideal honeymoon activity. I once asked Mrs Yeats what the psychic and physical effects were. "Utterly exhausting," she said. "When I came to out of the trance I would burst into tears." From this somewhat dubious source—which in later years he came to think might be merely the impact of his own "subconscious" on that of his wife—Yeats had gradually edited and constructed a complete philosophy of the mortal lot, as philosophical say as Blake's prophetic books, but not very much more authoritative. Although the concentric insistences of traditional dogma may distress us by their pride, rigidity and wilful disregard of the weaknesses in the argument, the eccentric speculations of anarchic intelligence, even when they fascinate by their novelty, often prove disappointing when their novelty has worn off, and Yeats himself was to end by casting doubts on his own grandiloquent system.

But at this moment, this summer morning in Merrion Square in 1926, it was uppermost in his thoughts, and he was delighted to find some of his speculations confirmed from a wholly unexpected and unknown source. Ideas float in the air. Vishnu may not dream the world, nevertheless the Earth Spirit shows itself singularly receptive to certain trends of thought at certain times. Yeats was delighted to find that he and Spengler had sometimes used even the same illustrations—the pierced eye of the Roman statue, for instance, compared with the "blind" eye of the Greek.

Thanks to the author of *The Decline of the West* I had

created a good impression, and, to my surprise and pleasure, the poet invited me to dine with him the following night. It was clear that he wanted an opportunity to pursue our topic. He was in good fettle. We crossed the road and walked together as far as Clare Street, past the grey and dignified solidity of the National Gallery which gains so much by being set well back from the square behind a foreground of green grass. He had been seeing my work from time to time in the *Irish Statesman* and he remarked "Your verse is good. You have no clichés in it;" an observation which sent me away happy for the rest of the morning.

X

In the event I was lucky to dine with him. Next day I drove down to Co. Wexford with my father and sister in the latter's baby Austin. Coming back my sister suggested that my father should be allowed to take the wheel and see how he liked the car. The brake and accelerator were in reverse position to those on his own car, and when a vehicle suddenly backed out right across the road, in front of a public house in Loughlinstown, my father jammed on what he thought was the brake. The next thirty seconds are sharply engraved in memory. That part of my father's brain which was responsible for steering, achieved a *tour de force* of serpentine evolutions at about sixty miles an hour, threading its way round the obstruction—at one moment we were going straight for the wall—while another part, that which looked after his feet, was endeavouring to adjust itself to the idea that it was high time he took his foot off the accelerator. It was with a definite sense of gratitude to providence that I found myself going up the steps of 82 Merrion Square at twenty minutes past seven o'clock.

I have an idea that I had been asked to come early. Certainly on this or another occasion about the same time —perhaps some morning—entering the drawing-room upstairs I found the poet leaning out of the window talking unconcernedly down into the garden below, and was given the impression, as with so much that he did, that he was staging himself, wished to appear unaware and yet was perfectly conscious that I was in the room all the time. In this I possibly wronged him.

The visit went off well. There was one fellow-guest at dinner, an American lady who does not figure very sharply in memory and was taken off by Mrs W. B. when we went upstairs later in the evening. Then at half-past eight A. E., Gogarty, Walter Starkie and E. R. Dodds, the biographer of Stephen MacKenna, joined us.

It was an historic occasion in Yeats's life. Crossing the room to a side-table he smote with his open hand on a great white stack of typescript and exclaimed "It is finished at last. The final page was typed this morning. There you see seven years' work."

He held up the bundle for us to see and we were duly impressed at the sight. We knew that Yeats had been at work on his contribution to philosophic thought for a long time. It bore little relation to orthodox philosophy. The poet was fond of lamenting his lack of scholarship. He would cross to his bookcase in search of a volume and loudly regret the fact that he had no intellectual training, "I am not educated." It might be truer to speak of *A Vision* as esoteric speculation rather than philosophy. Nevertheless it represented long periods of arduous work. When he first began it, Hone reminds us, "he was told by the communicators that the system of symbolism which awaited expression would take many years to become clear."

Hone has dealt admirably with the whole question of this book, as with so much else. He quotes from letters of both A. E. and F. P. Sturm on the subject of its personal psychological interest and its scholastic blunders.* I shall not venture into the maze now, but it was interesting to have been present on the day when—as he imagined—his toil had been completed. In fact the first edition of the book was only the prelude to extensive further labours and to the disclosure of the fact that the raw material for it, so to speak, had come via Mrs Yeats in trance.

Yeats rejoined us by the fire and announced that he

* *W. B. Yeats 1865–1939*, pp. 406–7.

82

doubted whether the critics would be able to make anything of it. It would be completely outside their province, and he chuckled to think of their predicament. A. E. believed that they would show extreme caution and would hedge, in so far as it lay in their power to do so. Nearly a year later, after the book had appeared, Yeats was writing to Mrs Shakespear: "*A Vision* reminds me of the stones I used to drop as a child into a certain very deep well. The splash is very far off and very faint. Not a review except one by A. E. . . . and no response of any kind except from a very learned doctor in the North of England who sends me profound and curious extracts from ancient philosophies on the subject of gyres." *

A. E.'s own review when it appeared seemed to me a masterpiece of tactful caution. It is reprinted in *The Living Torch* but, when I turn to it there and re-read it now, I realise that Russell showed more courage than I thought he had done. Its opening sentences are candid enough:

Here I fall away from a mind I have followed, I think, with understanding, since I was a boy, and as he becomes remote in his thought I wonder whether he has forgotten his own early wisdom, the fear lest he should learn "to speak a tongue men do not know." I allow myself to drift apart because I feel to follow in the wake of Yeats's mind is to surrender oneself to the idea of Fate and to part from the idea of Free Will. I know how much our life is fated once life animates the original cell, the fountain from which the body is jetted, how much bodily conditions affect or even determine our thought, but I still believe in Free Will and that, to use the language of the astrologers, it is always possible for a man to rise above his stars.

This is categorical, and it is followed by several pages of close reasoning before A. E. administers his spoonful of jam. It is possible, he then says, that *A Vision*

may be discussed feverishly by commentators a century hence, as Blake's prophetic books—so ignored, so unintelligible a

* F. P. Sturm.

83

hundred years ago—are discussed by many editors in our time, and he is found to be the profoundest voice of his own age. It is possible it may come to be regarded as the greatest of Yeats's works. It is conceivable also that it may be regarded as his greatest erring from the way of his natural genius, and the lover of his poetry may lament that the most intense concentration of his intellect was given to this book rather than to dramas or lyric. Personally, I am glad it was written. I do not doubt that though the seeds of his thought do not instantly take root and fructify in my mind they will have their own growth, and later I may find myself comprehending much that is now unintelligible.

It is possible that posterity may behave in the way suggested, but it is not probable. Blake's prophetic books have stimulated imaginations in our time, but they have not created any intellectual revolution. And, though the guesses of a genius are always valuable, the guesses of a genius who is opium-soaked, as Coleridge sometimes was, or who has been dancing attendance on the tricksy inhabitants of the spiritualistic world, or on the occult speculations of a MacGregor Mathers, as Yeats had, must be treated with some reserve. Yeats was like a man standing on the edge of an immense Alpine precipice and claiming every now and then, despite the wheeling and whirling mists, to have caught a brief glimpse of some landmark, some pinnacle of rock or green valley in the general murk below. There is always the possibility that he is right. But the conditions make verification impossible. Suppose the mist to lift, we might cry "Exactly! There is the village on the ledge just as he describes it." Or we might have to say "Hallucinations! There are no chalets at all at that spot; there is nothing but the bare rock."

A. E.'s review was very welcome. Macmillan's sent it out as a circular letter to the booksellers and it was shown to me in this form by Davis, the manager of Brentano's bookshop in Paris. A. E. had admitted that he found *A Vision* puzzling, but he was not intolerant:

As I looked at the diagrams and tables, so difficult to relate to life, I encouraged myself to explore by remembering what Neander wrote in his *Church History* when he was confronted by the task of elucidating the bewildering mythology of the Gnostics. We must remember, he said, that the mind of man is made in the image of God, and therefore even in its wildest speculations it follows an image of truth. That is, there is something in the very anatomy of the soul which prohibits its adventure into that which is utterly baseless and unrelated to life.

Of all my several evenings in company with Yeats this was the pleasantest one. His Monday evening was a restricted affair, altogether unlike A. E.'s crowded Sunday evening salon. I only once remember meeting Yeats at the latter and then he seemed a little out of place, unable to relax, unable to condescend and feel himself part of the homely intimacy and loquaciousness of that gathering. A. E.'s weekly at home was a democratic affair, distinctly bourgeois and animated enough to be French. You met all ages and all types. Yeats's Monday had an aristocratic touch about it, in keeping with the lovely room where it was held, but it drew upon a much narrower circle, either because the poet was too awe-inspiring, or because he limited his invitations. The only people that I can remember meeting there are Gogarty, Walter Starkie, A. E., Lennox Robinson, Lyle Donaghy, E. R. Dodds and Con Curran.

Dodds was present that night, and presently Lennox Robinson broke it to him that his fine poem "When the Ecstatic Body Grips" was one of two that had had to be omitted from the forthcoming school edition of his *Golden Treasury of Irish Verse*. Dodds made no complaint, he was the first to agree that it was hardly reading for the adolescent. But the thorny topic of literary censorship, official and unofficial, had been introduced, and in an entry in my journal a few months later I record that Yeats

becomes very indignant over what he thinks is an infringement of the liberty of thought or speech. Hence his feud with the

Roman Catholics . . . A member of some Roman Catholic Order has burnt "The Ballad of the Cherries," and going to his bookcase Yeats gropes about for his *Oxford Book of Ballads* and when found he searches through its pages for the ballad in question. He then chants it to us in a rich deep voice, stressing the metre strongly and reading more beautifully than I have ever heard ballad poetry read.

Both A. E. and Yeats chanted their own and other people's poetry in a unique way. Obviously as young men they had formed each his own theory on the subject, to which they still adhered. It was not a theory for general consumption and was chiefly successful because the manner so obviously fitted the man. A. E. chanted in long rolling periods with an occasional unexpected stress in an unmistakable Armagh brogue. He would beat time with a barely perceptible motion of his plump right hand, holding his pipe in his left, and fixing you with his penetrating eyes behind their steel-rimmed glasses, as though he wished you to realise that the recitation of poetry is always an act of ritual. Yeats might recite standing, coming down with bold emphasis upon every stressed phrase as well as emphasising the metre. He had no wish to speak poetry apologetically as though it were prose; poetry was in lines and the listener was entitled to have this brought home to him. His voice was more deliberate and more resonant than A. E.'s, and there was a challenge in it, in contrast with A. E.'s Brahminical detachment. If they had been anyone but themselves their audience would probably have burst into loud laughter; but because they were themselves the necessary reverence was forthcoming and one ended by finding the chanting a most moving experience.

I had given up my job in North Wales, found another for the autumn in an English school in Switzerland, and proposed to spend the three intervening summer months wandering, first in France, and then on a tour through Ireland with my parents. Now, in front of the wood-fire in

86

Yeats's grate, I happened to mention a vague plan that I had in mind, of going out to Fontainebleau when I got to Paris and perhaps joining the esoteric community that Gurdjieff had founded there. I knew very little about it save that Katherine Mansfield had gone there towards the end of her life and professed to have found the peace she was seeking; and that Orage, the brilliant editor of the *New Age*, had given up all his journalistic activities and submitted to its discipline. A. E. announced that the discipline imposed on Orage, the moment he arrived there, was to cart dung. Yeats thought this was a strange discipline for anyone in search of esoteric enlightenment; but A. E. explained to us, what Orage had already expounded to him, that it was all part of a carefully planned system to reduce the predominant influence of the conscious mind and give the subconscious mind a chance to function. Loading dung onto a cart was just the sort of thing to pacify the conscious mind, when it had become stirred into too much activity by intellectual gymnastics or trivial preoccupation with the external world. The dungcart brought it down to earth where it needed to be; the physical exercise calmed and strengthened the nerves, and Gurdjieff showed his great good sense in prescribing just this for a penitent intellectual. It not only achieved the needed result but also set a farm-hand free for other work. Someone pointed out that Orage had not remained in the community, but had gone off to America where there was hardly any horse-manure to cart, thanks to the discovery of the internal combustion engine. A. E. insisted that Orage had told him that he found the Fontainebleau retreat a wonderful experience and of great benefit.

In Jersey I had found a few hours of weeding a garden path distinctly calming to the nerves and, remembering Kipling's adumbrations on the subject, I was not one of those who laughed at Orage's experience. The talk passed to Katherine Mansfield and thence to Middleton Murry, her husband, and his abilities as a critic, and after some more literary discussion A. E. rose and said that he must catch his tram.

If it was time for his tram it was time for my and Robinson's last train. Yeats accompanied us to the door of the drawing-room. I was the last to leave. The other two were already descending the stairs when there took place an incident which has always remained in memory as a unique example of human feeling in a man who normally seemed too aloof to reveal it. For a moment—for a brief moment— he ceased to pontificate and spoke on a note of kindly human concern. The poet paused in the doorway, still holding the handle of the door, and, stopping me as I went out, said in a low earnest voice of great sincerity:

"Take the advice of an old man. Don't join that community at Fontainebleau. I have had a lot of experience of that kind of thing in my time, and my advice to you is— leave it alone. I know how such sects become priest-ridden and fall into the hands of charlatans. You are a young man and ought to be careful. I know what I am talking about."

I thanked him. I was the more moved because his action was so unexpected. What he had just said ran counter to much in his past life. The man who was telling me this had sat at the feet of Madame Blavatsky, established contact with MacGregor Mathers, and been initiated forty years before into the Golden Dawn, an order of Christian Cabalists. Both he and the young Russell had hoped much from the various cliques and circles of their youthful days. Hone sums up excellently the difference in outlook between the two men:

Russell believed that by the practice of austerities and concentration he could develop faculties of power over himself and a superior insight into Nature, but thought the attempt to compel men or non-human spirits to do one's will wrong and irreligious. This is, indeed, the rough distinction between mysticism and magic, for in magic, though it is the oldest form of religion, there is, as Hegel observes, no question of worship or of reverence for a spiritual being, for what has an absolute objective existence of its own. The process is rather the exercise of lordship over Nature—the sway of the magician over those who do not know: in short, all magic is black magic.

And now here was Yeats, in a moment of concern for a younger man, repudiating, it seemed, all his former attachments to Rosicrucians and others, and advising me to give such people a wide berth. The more inconsistent it might appear to be, the more well-disposed on his part it clearly was. I cannot remember what I said or whether I said anything at all, but the incident was to stick in memory long afterwards as evidence of kindliness in a man not greatly given, at least in my experience, to the manifestations of what one might call the homely virtues.

XI

WHEN I got to France a few weeks later I did not join the community in Fontainebleau—there was no community to join—but I took the train from Paris and paid a visit to the château where Orage had laboured so assiduously. Gurdjieff had been involved in a motor accident and had broken his leg. The Institute was in temporary abeyance: the only two disciples left were a very serious-looking young man, with sandy hair, from the English midlands, and a young girl with flaming red hair from America. They were both in their early twenties, slightly lost lambs, typical of hopeful, questing youth in search of the philosopher's stone. Fate and their own aspirations had brought them there and they now appeared to be stranded after, it was carefully explained to me, the ship had been only very temporarily grounded. They were making themselves useful and awaiting the moment when a more friendly tide would refloat the vessel. Gurdjieff could not teach his pupils with a broken leg. I was left to infer that he had dismissed them, or that they had slipped away one by one. The great man was upstairs in bed writing a book of enormous importance. I enquired its title and was told that it was probably to be called *Beelzebub's Talks to his Grandchildren*. This seemed to me an odd title, but the young man explained to me that Gurdjieff liked to surprise and even to shock his pupils by the novelty of his language, and that Beelzebub (presumably Gurdjieff) would have quite a lot of importance to say to his numerous grandchildren. In the absence of disciples, and of the teacher himself, the young man seemed to feel that the Institute needed defending. He showed me round, produced a lengthy printed form used to classify newly arrived patients or disciples, with spaces for almost every imaginable entry, from height, weight and blood pressure to the results of a careful psychoanalysis. One got the impression that Gurdjieff's system had incorporated the best of every other system as well. The young man kept stressing to me how happy Katherine Mansfield had been here in the closing days of her life. "She used to say all the time that she had never been as happy before—it was peace, absolute peace after the world she had been used to"—and presently he took me off to show me the Hall of Religious Dancing. We crossed the park to a low indeterminate building among the dripping trees. "It's not quite finished yet." That was only too evident. The interior suggested a Turkish bath that had fallen on evil days. Someone had whitewashed the walls and strewn a few worn carpets about the floor. Someone else had begun a series of garish, oriental wall-decorations which had not got very far. Despite the brightness of the colours an air of intolerable melancholy streamed from those uneven white surfaces, those brilliant garish blues and sombre reds. The interior was unfinished and, one felt, would never be finished. The idea was good; dancing is not without its religious significance. But it seemed certain that no genius of the dance would ever perform here, evoking emotions of reverence for the plastic beauty of the created form; that no-one at all would perform because the whole thing was only one more half-baked good intention, without the means or the talent to carry it out. I looked at it sadly, the young man looked at it sadly, and we then made our way back to the château where the mysterious author of *Beelzebub's Talks to his Grandchildren* was labouring in some distant bedroom, setting down the ideas which would enlighten mankind.

Established religions labour under many inconveniences and suffer from many faults, but they have this advantage:

although they may have lost much of their original ardour and sincerity, they have at least pruned away many of the extravagances which are liable to accompany the birth of a new faith; they know where they stand as regards morals; and they are purged of any terrible heresy which may at some time have tempted them to see in religion a short cut to the acquisition of personal power. Religion is not the deification of an individual will, it is "the flight of the Alone to the Alone," the search for that Divine Purpose which transcends our egocentric schemes. The portrait which Rom Landau paints of Gurdjieff in *God is my Adventure* is a far from attractive one, and I have been told other stories still less to his credit but which I do not feel justified in quoting, since I have not verified the facts in French legal records, if in fact they are to be found there. But my visit to Fontainebleau, so far from giving the lie to Yeats's forebodings, fully confirmed them. I had no wish to be weighed, tested, analysed, given a course of calisthenics, against the depressing background of what looked like a bankrupt Turkish bath, and finally made to listen to what Beelzebub had to say to me. It was almost with a sense of relief that I found myself once more on a very hard wooden seat in a third-class railway carriage on my way back to Paris.

The next three months were spent wandering by myself in France and then on a tour with my parents around the south and west coast of Ireland. Presently we came to Sligo. There I saw the massive, blocked-out form of Ben Bulben, silhouetted against the sky, a great right-angle of a mountain, flat-topped, sheer, a mountain that one day I would have as a constant companion, seen across the twenty intervening miles of Donegal Bay from the windows of the cottage in which we lived at Fintragh. I was in the Yeats country, and the curious thing was that I felt far nearer in spirit to the poet there than when I stood beside him in his own drawing-room.

What had happened to the man that he seemed so alien

to his own beginnings? And in any case why should one hold that against him as a crime? Other men's lives are not entirely consistent. Even my own well-loved father had changed. One of my half-sisters tells me stories of her childhood which suggest that my father, the black-bearded, puritanical curate who married a young widow with four children, altered nearly as much as Yeats in the course of the years, until he became the tolerant understanding individual we knew.

My father mellowed. Yeats seemed to have grown more harsh with the years, and to have slain the gentle idealist that he had once been. But he never abandoned his loyalty to the scenes of his youth. "Certain woods at Sligo, the woods above Dooney Rock and those above the waterfall at Ben Bulben, though I shall never perhaps walk there again, are so deep in my affection that I dream about them at night." His last poem was "Under Ben Bulben." Almost his last wish was that his bones should rest in Drumcliff churchyard. He was a man of more than fifty when he wrote, "When we are dead, according to my belief, we live our lives backwards for a certain number of years, treading the paths that we have trodden, growing younger again, even childish again, till some attain an innocence that is no longer a mere accident of nature, but the human intellect's crowning achievement." It is what the young girl had once said to him, but he has amplified it and spoilt it. As for the theory that we re-create our lives again, like so much in Yeats's thought it came out of the rag-bag of Madame Blavatsky's gleanings and speculations. Between earthly incarnations the soul of man is supposed to pass into a mental world of its own creation in which it evokes all that held its loyalty here on earth. The good man will be able to see the scenes, the friends, the relations that were dear to him, creating around himself a paradise of his own subjective imagining: the evil man will be at the mercy of his own dark thoughts. The idea is distasteful; there is something unsatisfactory in this doctrine of a completely subjective existence, a sort of glorified dream which seems real but in fact is self-projected by the individual himself to keep him occupied for a few centuries until he is ready to put on earthly vesture once more. If we are to meet those whom we love, in another existence, let them be real persons, not accommodating figments of our own creative fantasy. The occultists of the 1890's liked to have all the answers. Sometimes it was Indian metaphysics which they summoned to their aid, that great attempt of the human mind to relate microcosm to macrocosm. But, as likely as not, it was some obscure student of the Cabala, whose theories, liberally peppered with a few fancies of their own, they chose to serve up for the edification of the elect.

In Sligo I felt nearer to Yeats, far nearer than when I climbed the stairs in Merrion Square and came face to face with the man himself. Towards the end of the summer I went to stay with a brother-in-law in Connemara. Driving a ponytrap back from one of the beaches near Roundstone I allowed the wheel to mount a great granite boulder at the side of the narrow sandy lane, the trap turned over, the pony kicked clear of the broken shafts and galloped away and I found myself lying on the bank with my left arm curiously limp. The local doctor was a drunkard and my relatives would not let him lay a finger on me. Ranjit-sinhji's nephew from Ballynahinch drove to Clifden in search of the man there. For two and a half hours I lay in agony. My shoulder was dislocated and though, when the doctor at last arrived, it was the simplest thing for him to set it, the nerve had been nipped for so long that I had lost the use of my arm. I hastened back to Dublin to learn from my own doctor that the arm might always be paralysed. The next few weeks were spent trying by every means to restore life to it, and it was a proud moment when with my hand laid flat on the table I found one day that I could just slightly raise one of my fingers.

All this meant the suspension of literary contacts, though it was largely thanks to the skill of a fellow-writer, Winifred Letts, who had trained during the war as a masseuse, that I was able to travel out to my new post in Switzerland in the middle of September, albeit with one arm in a sling. I had not visited Rathgar Avenue before leaving, nor had I seen W. B. Any news I had of him came from Lolly.

XII

BOTH the Yeats sisters wrote to me from time to time and I have kept a number of their letters. Lolly was the more frequent correspondent in these earlier days. Her letters are always slightly chaotic and yet full of her own intense vitality. She could be sympathetic. Aware that I was unhappy in my first teaching job in North Wales she wrote: "I hope school is not too great a burden—the early part of the term is the worst—I even hate starting my painting classes again—but now the start is over I enjoy them—20 children of *all* ages from 6 to 16 and even a few grown-ups in one class."

She had taken another short poem of mine for her series of cards. Soon afterwards she sent me a rough pull of the illustration. Like all vehement personalities she was inclined to resort to underlining in her letters as a substitute for the emphasis she would have employed if she had been speaking.

I send the block-maker's rough proof—you will see that we mean to use it *as a small wall-picture as well*—so we really must pay you for it later when we are not so hard up. Do send the address of the U.S.A. man who buys first editions—I have *Insurrections*—I am not sure if it is a 1st ed.—it is not in paper —I will look it up and I am so hard up—I am trying to sell my own personal set of Cuala books. 37 volumes almost all autographed, and A. E. has written a poem in one, and John Eglinton also wrote in his *Essays*—and the first book of all *Seven Woods* has little marginal paintings by A. E. and others —the difficulty is I want *a good price*, they are "as new" and all have my signature and bookplate . . . I do envy you your trip to Rome, Capri etc.

What about your book? If you had seen W. B. he might have done a foreword. Don't say I *said this* but Mrs Yeats opens and does his letters for him—and anxious to save him work might not have produced yours at a good moment. *Don't* repeat this— she just casually mentioned it when we were going upstairs after lunch and said, "You never write introductions do you? Will I answer that?" "Yes," said W. B.—quite vague *I think* as to who had written asking for an introduction for their book. Burn this. I would not tell you, only *again* if you want his advice etc. see him yourself—and don't tell the home people— it might come round to George who is as good as gold—only wants to save W. B. work—but it is a hint for *again*. I even find no use writing notes. I *must see him* on any business.

Everything she says here, all the stresses and under- linings, the explosive staccato epistolary style, the method of punctuation—a quick series of dashes like the quick short pauses for breath when Lolly was talking to you—all this is extremely characteristic. I had forgotten completely the project for the book and my request for an introduction until I rediscovered this letter which Lolly had wished me to burn. A friend in the Channel Islands had suggested that I should get my poems set up and printed by a firm in Guernsey whose charges were remarkably low. This roseate prospect occupied me for a time. But long before anything was in train the cost of printing had gone up even in St Peter's Port, and the scheme had become impracticable.

In my pastoral valley in the Canton de Vaud, with vivid green fields outside the window and the jangle of cowbells in my ears, I was more than ever dependent upon the weekly arrival of the *Irish Statesman* to keep me in touch with the literary scene in Ireland. There I encountered most of my contemporaries, Clarke, O'Faolain, O'Connor, Higgins, McGreevy; and a number of my seniors. Not Yeats, for he very seldom contributed to his friend's paper. I can only remember one such contribution. If one met him in the columns of the *Statesman* it was because A. E. had written an illuminating review of his latest book. Russell could display considerable tact and even a certain degree of downright caution when writing of W. B. But his innate truthfulness always managed to say what it wanted to say in the end. Take for example all the various implications of this passage from his review of Yeats's collected *Essays*:

I spoke of this book as the only important contribution anyone had yet made to an Irish philosophy of literature and the arts, and yet there is no definite philosophy, the unity of the thought arising from the peculiar temperament or imagination of the poet rather than from any logical system he has thought out, and into which all must fit or be outcast. It is much better as it is, for the intuitions of a poetical nature are more exciting and profound than any logical philosophy of literature could be. We find what seem to be contradictions, but these are the natural reactions we find in ourselves from all our moods. We do not betray our ideals when we react from them, if we react with full consciousness, giving good reasons for our new departure. We have always to strike a balance between our own opposites, and the wisest thinker is he who is conscious that our nature is made up of opposing elements, all necessary, and who will not be afraid of speaking now from one pole of his being and now from another.

How tactful and how persuasive that is. It flatters Yeats's judgments which were generally thrown off arrogantly and impatiently, and with no suggestion that they were only separate facets of a multiple truth. It is almost too kind, for a thinker's first business is to make sure that he is not predicating irreconcilables. But Yeats resented every attempt to narrow the field. He had learnt from Blake to rage at all systematised thought. When in 1891 he was working on his edition of Blake we find him writing to Katharine Tynan that his Magnum Opus grows "more and more intricate and I hope more and more profound every day. The mystics all over the world will have to acknowledge Ellis and myself among their authorities."

98

But actually his Blake studies merely infected him with a liking for vague chaos. Both men were poets and not philosophers. Their irritation with established religions and philosophic systems was not solely because they were aware of the weakness in certain pretensions, but also because they themselves concealed an immense metaphysical arrogance, and had systems of their own—related in some measure, as Kathleen Raine has pointed out, to a general occult doctrine—to which they tried unsuccessfully to give cohesive expression.

Reading the *Irish Statesman* in a narrow bed-sitting room at the top of a huge wooden chalet in Château d'Oex kept me in touch with Ireland, as well as occasional brief letters from A. E. commenting upon some contribution I had sent him. I had reviewed both Keyserling and Spengler at some length in the *Statesman* and presently I was to have the pride and pleasure of seeing a notice of my own first book in the same columns. The prose poems from the *Fortnightly Review* and the *Spectator*, together with a number of others, had been gathered in 1926 into a small book and set up and printed on his handpress in Winchester by Alister Mathews whom I had met in the course of my travels. He had already published several books and Lolly's only complaint against him (she had been asked to send out notice cards of the book to her own clients) was that he was undercutting:

Your friend has sent me a sheaf of cards very nicely done too —announcing your book—and I *will* send them out to likely people—I have already sent nearly all—BUT and this a big *but*, how *can* a hand-printed book, sold for 3/-, pay? It is awkward because people will think *we* are profiteering—and we cannot make a book pay under 10/6—Mr Mathews is probably doing it *himself for fun*! ! There is not so much fun in twenty years of it —but we are doing better now—but if people produce books for 3/- it may injure us—he probably has no rent to pay—no wages etc. etc. I pay £10 a week in wages—so you see! Good luck to your book in any case.

Money was a perennial difficulty. A week before this she had written:

Lily starts off for England to-night via Liverpool and will be about a month on holiday—there is to be a Cuala Sale [at the] Lyceum Club on the 29—but Mrs Atkins (an Irish lady) and Hilda of the club will practically do it for her. I have got W. B.'s last book [presumably *A Vision*] far too dear—I am very hard up—and I want a really big sum for my Cuala set, £170. I have asked £180 and *may* end by taking £100. . . . I hope for a wealthy American but most people want only part of the set—and I must keep it together. Thank you for bookseller's address— I have written I have *Insurrections* and *The Crock of Gold* and lots of W. B., but those I mean to keep. I may be driven to sell.

Apparently I had showed myself sympathetic and had suggested doing something about the undercutting, for she writes shortly afterwards:

Good of you to think of the effect on us of advertising a book as *hand-printed at* 3/- *post free*—but I think that is too altruistic —after all it is Mr Mathews' affair—only I do *know* if he paid for labour and royalties etc.—or even charged up *his own time* against it—3/- couldn't pay. A. E. is on holiday but I expect he will soon be back—his son Dermot is now Sub-Editor—and he wrote me a note and said his father was away. W. B. is up from Galway for 2 days—they came up for Senate and to fetch Anne and Michael down with them to the Castle. Anne has done a wonderful (I think) painting from the window here [Cuala Industries were now installed at 133 Lower Baggot Street in Dublin, Lolly coming in daily from Churchtown] of this builder's yard—I will send it to the R.D.S. and hope she will again get a prize—I suppose she can get it two years running— she is 7 and 4 months and so still goes in with the children 6–8. She is a *wonderful observer*—sees *everything at a glance*—and *can put it down*—like someone with *inherited knowledge* of drawing —not a bit like any child of seven I ever taught before. She has not to catch her interest by pretty colour etc.—it is apparently the *form itself* that thrills her. I think Mr Mathews is very clever to get the book done at all—printing one page at a time. We print 4 and could do more.

I was at the College Races yesterday—a lovely day and a fine crowd. It *felt more like* old times—more sociable and the people *looked much better*, very well dressed and gay—but I hear the Provost is ill again—I hope not serious—Dr L. C. Purser took his place yesterday.

We are going to tea with Mrs Verschoyle today.

Yours affectionate cousin
Elizabeth C. Yeats.

When the book appeared she welcomed it generously.

I am delighted with *The Tremulous String*—it has just come —I don't know yet what I like best. "The Last Thing," "He Regrets that his First Memory of her is lost," and "Phelim's child kisses him," all are lovely and appeal to me, but as yet I have not had much time to really enjoy the book—it is nicely printed but his margins are not good.

And she went on to draw a picture of what margins should really be.

A few months later she writes:

I sent *The Trembling* [*sic*] *String* to Dr Louis Purser at Christmas and he seemed greatly pleased with it—he said when he wrote, "W. M. Gibbon's prose poems are certainly very beautiful in expression and rhythm, though I think they would never stick in one's memory the way verse does?" He has a wonderful memory for verse—I wish *I* had.

I can find few letters from Lily Yeats at this time. Either there were none, or I have mislaid them. But there is one dated 23 January 1926. I must have told her of a recent visit to Taormina and of how I had promised to lecture to an English-speaking literary society in Château d'Oex on W. B., but would have to depend upon a Tauchnitz selection for the poems which I read them. Lily wrote:

Thank you so much for your letter. I also heard of your doings in Sicily—your father read me a letter of yours—very good one too. You are right about the Lily Gordon (Williams) portrait [I had been shown a painting by Mrs Leader-Williams

101

in Taormina of herself as a young girl, painted by John Butler Yeats in his studio in Dublin forty years before]. It was done in or about 1886, the same year as K. T.'s. It is a much better portrait I think—one of my father's best of that period—there is another very good one of the same time of George Coffey of the Museum. Dermot Coffey has it.

I hope your lecture on W. B. went off well. Write and tell me about it. I told him and he said some complimentary things of your verses, and also that he had only got £20 for the Tauchnitz but they are so terribly nice to you that you give them all they ask. He is well and hard at work—little Anne has been very ill with congestion of the lungs; at first they feared pneumonia but she is now herself again, gay and vivid. When I saw her yesterday she was dressed in cowboy trousers and having her tea—with lovely sugar cake—the kind we only got on birthdays—but children now get it everyday.

Do you see we are to have our own coins? [W. B. was to be chairman of the committee to choose the designs.] Now is the time for the churches to write and demand the total destruction of the 3d bit. There was an old parson near Sligo who tried to withdraw them—at his death £200 worth of them were found in his safe. My plan is better.

The lecture went off well to a fairly large audience gathered in the chalet rented by Lushington, an ex-master from Eton, for his coaching establishment. This was the second time I had lectured on W. B. The previous occasion was in Jersey and a lady had arrived then, having misread the small display notice in the local evening paper, and expecting to hear a lecture on Keats. She stayed, professing herself grateful afterwards to the alphabetical error which had brought her there. After the lecture she embarrassed me considerably by saying to me in intense tones "I want you to tell me something. What does it *feel* like to be a poet?" This is the sort of remark that is enough to make any poet goggle helplessly and wish that he could withdraw his head quietly like a tortoise behind the protection of a high collar. But my guardian angel must have been at hand. I rose to the occasion and replied instantly, with

102

almost Yeatsian dignity: "A pinprick to you is a sword-thrust to us."

In my journal I describe a visit paid to Yeats in this summer of 1926 when I had come back to Dublin on holiday. I had been away nearly a year, having spent the Christmas holiday in Sicily, where I met my future wife, and the Easter one in Rome and Naples.

When I return from Switzerland I go to see Yeats. I have sent him my book but he has taken no notice of it. But presently crossing the room he sits down beside me and says, "I see you have published a book since I last saw you." I interrupt him, muttering "Yes," and go on hastily to say that I have spent Easter on Capri, from which I see part of his last book is dated, this from pride and because I have no wish for him to think that I had come there that night to extract an opinion he would not commit to paper.

When I read this now it seems to me that I was absurdly tetchy. I would have loved to hear his verdict; but no, he must not think that I had come there fishing for it. It is true that Yeats was chary of giving an opinion on the worth of younger poets and, later, he was to fly into a tremendous rage with Sheila Wingfield when, having praised her fine verses most generously and sincerely in a letter, he found that she had allowed her publisher to quote his opinion in print. We all knew that he was the opposite of A. E. in this respect. At the back of my mind therefore was probably a sense of mortification that even if he praised the poems now it would only be "off the record," and that it was perhaps caution that had prevented his putting pen to paper. In this I wronged him, as subsequent letters showed.

The same evening the talk turned presently to racial characteristics, and Yeats attacked hotly the view that it was the English public-schoolboy type who had produced the Empire.

"It is they on the contrary who are losing it," he declared

loudly, contending that rich characters like Clive and Warren Hastings were adventurers, cads almost; the complete antithesis of the hide-bound, unimaginative, class-prejudiced individual who had been going to India now for at least half a century. The doctrine of white superiority, he assured us, had to be bolstered up, and he went on to tell us the story of a man in Ceylon who, asked why he believed in making the natives leave the footpath to the white man, replied: "When we came here first the Englishman himself inspired the necessary respect by his own character; but now that they send us fools and strumpets, how else are you going to maintain prestige?"

He told the story with relish and bitterness, and the full flavour of his personality rises up in memory when I retell it now. I admired the caustic vigour of his speech and laughed with the others. Nevertheless much of Yeats's talk left an acrid taste in the mouth. I could enjoy the outrageously witty and occasionally blasphemous table-talk of Anatole France as recorded by his secretary Brousson;* I could forgive Moore the indecencies of *A Storyteller's Holiday*, which seemed only the exhibitionism of a naughty child fundamentally innocent at heart. But if Yeats chuckled over Gogarty's latest anecdote, my reaction was almost that of a young girl, shocked that her hero should have feet of clay. Why? Was it that Yeats was a poet, and that I was a young man fresh from a good deal of suffering in the war, anxious to discover a teacher who would dispense only sweetness and light? Was it that France's wit and Moore's improprieties seemed only surface traits, which concealed much underlying goodness and pity, whereas Yeats's anger was genuine and scabrous, the anger of a Lucifer whose scornful laughter echoes through the empty places of the universe? Moore had forgiven life, for the sake of its unquestionable beauty; France had found that he could temper its anguish, thanks to pity and

* Much of it apocryphal.

irony. But Yeats still raged, and it was pride and scorn, rather than solicitude for his fellow-men, which made him rage:

> I pray—for fashion's word is out
> And prayer comes round again—
> That I may seem, though I die old,
> A foolish, passionate man.

He cannot forgo his oblique taunt against prayer, but must make it in that caustic aside, before he utters the prayer itself, which, some would say, was to be answered in the years to come.

XIII

I WAS never at my best in his company. In fact I was always at my worst. The homage that I wanted to offer was always in the course of the evening tempered by some instinctive reflex of disapproval of the kind I have been describing. I had no use for other men's anger. I had had enough distress of mind of my own. Laotze, with his "gentleness is invisible," "to see things in the germ, that I call intelligence;" New Thought, with its assurance that by selecting our mental preferences we can actually influence the event; A. E. with his "we become what we contemplate"— that was the kind of gospel I had chosen, when I turned away from the despair that war and illness had threatened to induce in me. Yeats might dismiss von Hügel, albeit with blessings on his head, and claim:

Homer is my example and his unchristened heart,

but I found in von Hügel all the heroic patience of the sage, and Yeats's claim to kinship with Homer seemed wide of the mark. "Reverence chilled and irritated him," says Strong.

Never, in all the years that I knew him, was I to feel completely at ease with him. Never was I to feel that I was in contact with a fellow human being. "You are afraid of him, that's the real trouble," Lily Yeats once said to me. And she made it plain that this was the very worst approach of all; that though W. B. might like to inspire awe (she did not actually say this) nevertheless he hated and despised his awe-inspired victim. He liked people who could conquer their dread of him, stand up to him, take him with easy familiarity.

Stand up to him, but only in semblance, only in the fashion of an actor playing a part. I did stand up to him, but in wholly the wrong way. I argued with him. I cross-examined him on his ideas. I had this excuse that, living abroad, it was an intoxicating experience to come back to Dublin and its great talkers. I was full of reverence for the individual, but where ideas were concerned I cherished the firm conviction that no man's ideas were sacrosanct, and that even a great man must be prepared to defend the position he takes up, against the assaults of epigoni.

It was a fatal line to take with a man who hated all opposition. None of Yeats's personal friends in Dublin, except A. E., were philosophers or metaphysicians, and they tended to play up to him in a tactful way. A. E. avoided the controversial. He and W. B. had long ago clarified their individual differences—which were considerable—and there was no point in going over the ground again. Instead A. E. puffed away at his pipe. When Yeats encountered opposition it was generally from temperaments not dissimilar from his own, like Seumas O'Sullivan, or Austin Clarke or Thomas Bodkin, and the antagonism boiled quickly to a head. The offender, if he became troublesome, was cast into outer darkness, and that was the end of it.

It is misleading then to say that the poet liked people to stand up to him; any real conflict of will or of ideas irritated him. Yeats's friends did not stand up to him in any serious sense. Gogarty had an oblique technique of his own which was highly successful. Curran once said to me, "You know, I have a feeling that Yeats is afraid of Gogarty." Fred Higgins prided himself that he stood up to W. B., but this pious faith was largely compensatory. Certainly in one of his letters to Dorothy Wellesley Yeats announces complacently that Higgins has been avoiding him for days, being afraid to meet him, having given a vote contrary to his wishes at a meeting of the Academy of Letters. It would probably be true to say that W. B. liked an outward

107

show of boldness combined with a considerable degree of discriminatory tact; and this was just what I did not possess. My attitude was a mixture of awed reverence for so great a poet, and quick irritation at the capricious line liable to be taken by his thought.

A classic example of this caprice is when he declares in the introduction to his anthology that he has rejected certain poems because "passive suffering is not a theme for poetry." He explains: "In all great tragedies, tragedy is a joy to the man who dies." But such a sweeping generalisation invites debate. The grey-faced men whom I had seen waiting in the dusk at Suchez until it was dark enough to go up the line had had their fill of suffering both active and passive. A child, killed with the promise of life before it, is, according to this theory, not a tragic theme—"some blunderer has driven his car onto the wrong side of the road—that is all." It was this habit, acquired possibly from his father, of throwing out a controversial dictum and leaving it at that, which made intellectual contacts with Yeats so maddening. Who was this man that he should claim the right of utterance in the manner of the Pythian oracle? Even in his poetry his cryptic scorn can sometimes anger us.

A STICK OF INCENSE
Whence did all that fury come?
From empty tomb or Virgin womb?
Saint Joseph thought the world would melt
But liked the way his finger smelt.

There is a gibe here, but it is too subtle for most of us, which is perhaps just as well. Graves in his Clark Lectures says the lines are a *double-entendre* and "combine blasphemy with obscenity." Although I am not a Roman Catholic, they offend me, seeming to dismiss human piety with a sneer and a snigger. A. E. was not a Roman Catholic either, but how completely different was his technique. In his preface to a volume of verse by a young woman who had once been on the staff of his paper and whose work revealed marked traces of Catholic piety he wrote: "We see different eternities. This is not the heaven I would enter. These saints, these divinities are not those I worship . . . but I remember the year she was a literary colleague, how natural, kind and good she was, and if any word of mine could draw attention to the natural charm of her verses I gladly give it."

Yeats not only disliked his ideas being questioned; he was not markedly receptive to those of others. I said to him once: "I suppose if we were really philosophic, that is to say if we could contemplate the issue with the detachment which the philosophic mind should bring to all things, we should be able to banish personal feeling from our consideration of immortality. Even our own future destiny could not shake us out of that calm." He looked at me sharply from under disapproving brows and said: "I don't agree with you at all."

Occasionally he would say something so vivid that even my annoying cross-examination was brought to a sudden halt. Once I said to him in the course of some dispute, "Then you don't think that conduct matters at all?" "Nothing matters except the heroic mind." It was a superb reply and it silenced me. Nevertheless deep in my heart I knew that it had no philosophic significance. For the heroic mind itself is partly the product of vision, and partly the product of conduct and deliberate choice. One cannot isolate it in a vacuum. Virtue, as we know it, begins in right thinking and ends in right action, and it is only when we come to art that the heroic mind is its own vindication; for in art it is intensity that matters even more than direction.

I was young, opinionated and argumentative, but also genuinely in search of truth. I tended to approach every great man as a possible solution to all my intellectual and moral problems. I wanted a teacher. I wanted a *guru* to

109

whom I could be *chela*. At once sensuous and puritanical, sceptical and devout, I knew only one thing, that the good radiate their own justification. A. E.'s goodness turned aside the shafts of even his most convinced intellectual opponents. The goodness of Socrates, the goodness of The Old Boy (Laotze) infused their words with a significance which nothing else could give. But when I turned to Yeats for bread, he gave me a stone.

Even now when I read any passage of his prose concerned with ideas I tend to question it, to demand explanation and gloss. I refuse to let myself be carried away on some full-sailed sentence. There are times when it even seems to me that Yeats is the forerunner of the whole modern cult of the meaningless. Words are to impress, rather than to clarify and elucidate. Even science must learn to juggle skilfully with words, if it is to expect our homage. Against this linguistic humbug, pseudo-scientific, pseudo-psychological, pseudo-literary, we seem to be helpless, until fashion shall once more "come round again" and exalt the Latin genius and the virtues of clarity and lucidity. It was the German mind which first showed a taste for generalisation, and for all the perils of abstract jargon; but Yeats, with his stress on style and his love of the symbol, has probably done more than any man to popularise vague speech with those who use the Anglo-Saxon tongue.

It is possible of course to be unfair to him. Take this passage:

I still think that in a species of man, wherein I count myself, nothing so much matters as Unity of Being, but if I seek it as Goethe sought, who was not of that species, I but combine in myself, and perhaps as it now seems, looking backward, in others also, incompatibles. Goethe, in whom objectivity and subjectivity were intermixed, I hold, as the dark is mixed with the light at the eighteenth Lunar Phase, could but seek it as Wilhelm Meister seeks it, intellectually, critically, and through a multitude of deliberately chosen experiences; events and forms of skill gathered as if for a collector's cabinet; whereas true Unity

110

of Being, where all the nature murmurs in response if but a single note be touched, is found emotionally, instinctively, by the rejection of all experience not of the right quality, and by the limitation of its quantity.

This is not from *A Vision*: it is from *The Trembling of the Veil*, which was published in 1922. At first I experience a sense of annoyance that Yeats should play tricks with words and even juggle badly with them: "Goethe, in whom objectivity and subjectivity were intermixed;" "combine in myself, and perhaps as it now seems, looking backward, in others also, incompatibles." This is not the language of precise thought; in fact, in the second sentence, the meaning eludes me; I cannot see how Yeats can combine incompatibles in other people. It would be relevant to ask whether Goethe was in search of unity, or was his aim multiplicity for its own sake? It is only when I reach the close of the passage that I begin to admire the mind behind it. There the poet does make his point. Today, more than ever, it is necessary to select our experience, to withdraw in some degree from the periphery of consciousness, where the multiple events of the world threaten to overwhelm us, and to achieve that inner centrality which is perhaps the real purpose of life.

The passage is at least debatable; but with Yeats you were not allowed to debate anything. If you questioned his ideas, with the earnestness and pedantry of youth, you were outside the pale. A. E. listened to you patiently. Yeats swept you aside. And because my intellectual sympathies instinctively lay elsewhere, my questions tended to be just the sort which annoyed him.

He had entered public life at this time, accepting a seat in the Senate, whereas A. E. had refused one. This was a somewhat Goethean step, and did not tend towards unity of being. In the Senate he had made an impassioned speech against the bill which made divorce impossible in the Free State. He began it, Hone tells us, deathly pale, and he

111

finished it with sweat pouring from his brow. In the course of the speech he trod on every toe that offered. He saw himself on this occasion as the defender of Protestant liberties; nevertheless he cast doubt on the historical validity of the Gospels, speaking of them rather in the way a Gnostic would do, as symbol rather than fact. Once more it was a case of "back to Blavatsky." He gibed at the Irish puritan tradition—shared alike by Protestants and Catholics —and took a malicious delight in reminding his fellow-senators (several of whom left the House to show their displeasure) that the three bronze statues presiding over Dublin's chief thoroughfare were of men who had flouted the moral code. At this point Lord Glenavy, distressed by the direction which the speech was taking, cried: "Do you not think that we might leave the dead alone?" To which Yeats flashed back instantly: "I would hate to leave the dead alone."

He had not come to the Senate, Hone says, "to trail his coat. He was always a controversialist, but this was certainly an occasion when he spoke with conviction." It is true, but it is precisely as a controversialist—in his early controversy with A. E., in his controversy with Noyes, in his controversy with Bodkin—that he shows up so badly. His instinct was not to debate but to bludgeon or mock an opponent into silence, the instinct in fact of a timid and sensitive man, anxious to get the thing quickly over. But his opponents could not know that his arrogance was in some degree the obverse of a natural timidity. All they encountered was his scorn.

I remember the savage glee with which Yeats told us one night that there used to be a saying in the country that you could not throw a stone over a workhouse wall in Ireland without hitting one of Daniel O'Connell's children. Perhaps his fellow-senators were given the same anecdote. Certainly the combative streak, roused it should be noticed —another Blavatskian trait—on so many occasions by

112

other people's notions of piety, loved to strike home. The statues—of Nelson, Parnell and O'Connell—figured in a short poem as well as in the speech on divorce:

THE THREE MONUMENTS

They hold their public meetings where
Our most renownèd patriots stand,
One among the birds of the air,
A stumpier on either hand;
And all the popular statesmen say
That purity built up the State
And after kept it from decay;
Admonish us to cling to that
And let all base ambition be,
For intellect would make us proud
And pride bring in impurity:
The three old rascals laugh aloud.

Daniel O'Connell might have laughed aloud. But I cannot see either Nelson or Parnell doing so. They were only too anxious to maintain appearances. Nelson was not an Irish patriot, and the only real laughter in this piece of doggerel is Yeats's own rather harsh guffaw.

It was that scornful guffaw which I knew so well. It was not the whole man. It was only a small part of the man; and that in old age. Nevertheless it seemed to dominate the stage whenever I met him. There were other facets as well. There must have been. There was genuine humour, as in this extract from a letter to Mrs Shakespear, written in 1928 when he was just back from convalescence in Rapallo:

Two Dublin doctors have sat upon me; the Cannes man said "Lungs and nervous breakdown can be neglected, nothing matters but blood pressure," and gave me a white pill. The Monte Carlo man said "Blood pressure and lungs can be neglected, nothing matters but nervous breakdown," and gave me a brown pill. The Dublin men said "Blood pressure and nervous breakdown can be neglected, nothing matters but lungs," and have given me a black pill, and as a sort of postscript I am to have a vaccine injection once a month for the next three months.

There was kindness and goodness of heart, as in his advice to me about the institute at Fontainebleau, or in an early letter to A. E. where he shows personal concern for his friend, urging him not to take the risk of giving up the post he had thought of abandoning, but the dominant impression of the later Yeats—and it is to be found in the poems too—was one of *hauteur*, irascibility and a proud detachment. At all times he remained something of a mystery. I could not have put words to this feeling. He did not seem an unhappy man, he seemed rather a man overwhelmingly impressive, but at the same time concealing behind a façade, which he himself had gradually and deliberately built up, whole areas of consciousness. One could never penetrate his defences. They were the work of a lifetime.

Lennox Robinson acquits him of pretentiousness, saying that we hear often of an unbuttoned Beethoven, but "there was no unbuttoned Yeats, either in his work or in himself, and that is why I deny that he was guilty of pose." It is a subtle defence, but a little like saying that a person must not be accused of climbing onto a pedestal because it is his natural habitat and he lives there. L. A. G. Strong's defence is a little different. He rebuts the charge of arrogance. "Sociable and a talker he preserved his personality from the attrition of casual contacts . . . It was a popular delusion that Yeats was aloof and incapable of warmth and friendship . . . True, the poet was not for all comers. 'There is not a fool can call me friend . . .' He could magisterially resent a liberty, and the uninvited stranger was soon shown the door."

This is obviously sincere, but it is in some way special pleading. Casual contacts are admittedly a menace to the writer; but many writers have worked out a technique which will avoid hurting feelings unduly. Yeats was in-

114

capable of such a technique. Perhaps it was because he was shy; perhaps because he was overbearing.

Sitting in front of the gas-stove in Jack Yeats's studio one evening I hinted to him that W. B.'s manner to the world was a trifle arrogant. He murmured something in his brother's defence. I cannot recall the exact words, but they were to the effect that the rebuffs and snubs and financial struggles of youth had left their mark on him, and were the real explanation of the *hauteur* with which he now confronted the world.

Many people in Ireland were content to separate the poetry and the individual. His verses were one matter: Yeats was another. But this was just what I could not do. For I held the view that the poet is always the real man, that whatever is deepest and most valuable in personality finds utterance in the moment of inspiration. A man is not less himself when he writes poetry; he is more himself. We must seek him there, if we are to find the reality. This self, it is true, is a kind of over-self; but then the over-self is the real self, even though it may find its voice only in the fore-ordained moment.

But Yeats had moved away from his over-self. He was even hostile to the poet he had been in youth. His art was still everything to him, but he had found a new Muse and turned his back on the old. This inner revolution—almost as great as that which made Rimbaud turn away from poetry altogether—might excite the plaudits of novelty-mongers, but it could mean that he had moved away from his true centre. At any rate, in the man the impression which it gave was that of a soul at war with itself.

I was too young then to know how far we all move away from ourselves. An A. E. may win slowly through to serene calm, turning all that he meets on the way to his own steadfast purpose. A Walter de la Mare may continue whimsical and humble and affectionate to the end. But in other natures the poet has been able to take possession only

115

at certain moments; he has said his say, making utterance from the depths of his being, and then the man has returned to eat husks.

Years later, not with Yeats in mind at all, but thinking how of all my contemporaries Austin Clarke alone looked and acted the part of a poet, whereas other men almost gave the lie to their *métier*, I was to write:

POETS

Suddenly struck by a line
Stately-toned as a bell,
I think, "The metal is gold,
But the coin has been clipped to hell.
Meeting him in the street,
Is there smallest sign to say
Here a god dwelt and spoke
In a house of clay?"

Nothing. The joss-sticks burn
Incense before a mask.
More and more, poets grow
Less and less like their task.
Faces deteriorate,
Anxious, or prone to bask
In their own eyes' favour. "Where
Is the god?" I ask.

Vanished. And yet I know
Demi-god there must be
Who, from his battered shrine,
Utters oracularly.
This shell, like the other sort,
Echoes its native sea,
Murmurs of fields once green
And a spirit once free.

XIV

ONE of the things I disliked in W. B. was his assumed
pose of a man of the world, and his acceptance of bawdiness. There was something slightly unreal about it. It did
not suit him. I had lived in the army for three years and
was no sheltered flower where obscenity was concerned. But
when Gogarty arrived, jauntily rubbing his hands together
and with his latest dirty story already well-rehearsed, or
when Walter Starkie gleefully passed us on some *bon mot*
of the common room, and Yeats gave a raucous almost
forced guffaw of laughter, it made for me an instantaneously
unfavourable impression. Perhaps the presence of A. E. on
these occasions contributed in no small measure to this
result. He smoked away quietly, as it were oblivious to all
this; and if I looked towards him I saw his grey-green eyes
gleaming benevolently behind the steel-rimmed spectacles.
There sat the sage in almost Buddhistic detachment, and
Gogarty's stable-lane anecdote and Yeats's guffaw became
more irrelevant than ever. The more I tried to remember the greatness of my host, and the more I tried not
to criticise him even mentally, lest the vibrations of my
thought should, as it were, rebound from the walls—disapproval being, like enthusiasm, something which produces
its instantaneous facial manifestation, a tightening of the
corners of the mouth, a slightly more frozen look in the eyes
—the more I seemed to radiate my mood of condemnation.
It was priggish. It was, in a way, unfair. Strong is illuminating when he says that Yeats laughed at the dirty story
he had just told you but could be very quickly shocked if

117

you told him one in return. Many of us are like that. We draw the line where we think it should be drawn, shock others, but are immediately shocked ourselves when our own personal line is passed. A. E. was no prude, but he was steeped in idealism and would have thought it out of character to be amused by Gogarty's indecencies. His moral earnestness made it impossible. I remember one Sunday evening at Rathgar Avenue discussing with Arnold Marsh, the Quaker schoolmaster, the attitude of the different army commands, English, French and American, to the sexual problems of the soldier. The red lamp establishment was banned by the Americans; approved, one imagines, by the French; and condoned—with penalties of stopped leave for a year, if a visit to one brought distressing consequences —by the English. Suddenly A. E., out of the wreaths of smoke encircling him, cut into our conversation to say quietly, "I can understand a man being in love with a particular woman and desiring her—but promiscuity, no, I can't understand that."

Yeats was incapable of making such a remark. It would have been out of character, or out of present character. In my journal I noted: "He speaks as a Freudian," and then, anxious not to be unfair to him, "but he is a married man and it is difficult to know how much he means. His talk may just be a reaction against his own austere youth."

Part of the truth was that my admiration for the artist was so great that it was *lèse-majesté* for the man to fall short in any respect. I was judging him continually by the standards of his own superb achievement. A man who could write such lines as he had written should be above taunts and irascibilities, yet Higgins could warn a friend that W. B., if annoyed, could be malicious and vindictive. "Gentleness is invincible," but Yeats despised it, and boasted that he drew his inspiration from its opposite. Only in a rare moment of chastened repentance did he even attempt to excuse himself:

118

Out of Ireland have we come.
Great hatred, little room,
Maimed us at the start.
I carry from my mother's womb
A fanatic heart.

Once he might say what he wanted to say without ran-
cour, and allude to old age without actually baring his teeth.
And then what a poem is the result. He visits a convent
school in the south of Ireland, walks through the classes
accompanied by "a kind old nun in a white hood," feeling
himself "a sixty-year-old smiling public man." Suddenly
the sight of all these young faces reminds him of the
phoenix of his youth and of how she had once told him of an
incident in her own childhood which had filled her with a
child's sense of injustice:

I dream of a Ledaean body, bent
Above a sinking fire, a tale that she
Told of a harsh reproof, or trivial event
That changed some childish day to tragedy—
Told, and it seemed that our two natures blent
Into a sphere from youthful sympathy,
Or else, to alter Plato's parable,
Into the yolk and white of the one shell.

And thinking of that fit of grief or rage
I look upon one child or t'other there
And wonder if she stood so at that age—
For even daughters of the swan can share
Something of every paddler's heritage—
And had that colour upon cheek or hair,
And thereupon my heart is driven wild:
She stands before me as a living child.

Her present image floats into the mind—
Did Quattrocento finger fashion it
Hollow of cheek as though it drank the wind
And took a mess of shadows for its meat?

119

And I though never of Ledaean kind
Had pretty plumage once—enough of that,
Better to smile on all that smile, and show
There is a comfortable kind of old scarecrow.

The theme is age. But for once he is able to speak without bitterness and with only a rueful shake of the head. The memory of Maud Gonne, compelling his pity as a young man, as she sits beside him over a dying fire, has sweetened all; and the poem continues for four more magnificent stanzas, as serene as the great poem he had written for his daughter.

More than thirty years separated me from Yeats. I was young, chaste, sensual, priggish and intensely romantic. I held with Plato and Plotinus that love is the moment of revelation; it seemed to me that when we fall in love we see another human-being irradiated in supernal light, as God perhaps sees them; while in the same moment they, by the mere fact of being loved, become not less themselves but, by so much, the more so. As for the flesh, it could be hallowed by genuine passion, or by the semi-mystical approach of the Hindu or the Persian to bodily commerce. But that was a wholly different thing from the savage coarseness of Boswell or from "porter-drinkers' randy laughter."

In his later verse Yeats stresses the body, deliberately, and in contrast to all his earlier transports of soul:

Go your ways, O go your ways,
I choose another mark,
Girls down on the seashore
Who understand the dark;
Bawdy talk for the fishermen;
A dance for the fisher-lads;
When dark hangs upon the water
They turn down their beds.
          Daybreak and a candle-end.

He has travelled a long way since the day when he wished

120

MONK GIBBON, 1928

to spread the heaven's embroidered cloths beneath the feet of his beloved. When he wrote "The Wild Old Wicked Man" Yeats may have been thinking of some local, ragged byword, belonging to the days of his Sligo youth, but he was also, almost certainly, thinking of himself and, for that matter, of most of us. Which of us, looking across the room at a pretty girl and listening at the same time to a flood of prognostications from some political know-all, does not want to cry out, as Yeats has done in *Politics*,

> And maybe what they say is true
> Of war and war's alarms,
> But O that I were young again
> And held her in my arms!

The frankness of the later poetry is the frankness of Burns, though it may seem more appropriate on the lips of a younger man. I admire the superb vigour of "The Wild Old Wicked Man," but it is the final abandonment of all Plotinian sublimation:

> "Because I am mad about women
> I am mad about the hills,"
> Said that wild old wicked man
> Who travels where God wills.
> "Not to die on the straw at home,
> Those hands to close these eyes,
> That is all I ask, my dear,
> From the old man in the skies"
>> *Daybreak and a candle-end.*

The poem is a mixture of Villon and the Sligo of Jack Yeats; a manifesto of unslaked, unregenerate craving, but from a mind fully conscious that "All men live in suffering . . . whether they take the upper road or stay content on the low."

> "That some stream of lightning
> From the old man in the skies
> Can burn out that suffering
> No right-taught man denies.

121

> But a coarse old man am I,
> I choose the second-best,
> I forget it all awhile
> Upon a woman's breast."
> *Daybreak and a candle-end.*

"A young man in the dark am I, but a wild old man in the light," a wild old man, content with the second-best. It is public knowledge that Yeats went to some trouble—the trouble of a glandular operation—to be still assured of that second-best, and the literary experts have commented upon the renewed youth which they say his Muse shared with him. Some of the phallic allusions in The Lady and The Chambermaid series suggest a too great obsession with the physical; it is inconceivable to think of them figuring in *The Rose* which was published forty years before. Not only the man but the age had undergone a psychological transformation. The natural inclination of the human mind towards extremes, and its inability ever to strike a happy mean, has resulted, in our time, in a reaction out of Victorian prudery and excessive reticence into an almost obsessional preoccupation with the physical. A Persian poet can treat an erotic theme with frankness and yet reverence, because love still remains mysterious and a force to be reckoned with. But our semi-scientific, pseudo-psychological approach to the subject rejects love, affirms sex, and ends by seeming more interested in the aberrations of morbid individuals than in the normal and well-balanced.

Yeats is not decadent, but, just as Joyce seems permanently anchored in the indecencies of certain adolescent minds, so Yeats seems unable to get away from the physical preoccupations of later middle-age. Certain poets seem to be the forerunners and creators of the age which follows them, either because their influence upon its thought is so great that they may be said to shape it; or because their specialised sensitivity to intellectual atmosphere makes them receptive to an existent trend long before other men

122

are aware of it. It was almost an obsession with Yeats—the corollary possibly of some psychological revolution in himself—not to become stuck in the past, not to repeat himself, always to move forward to something new and different. And it was a revolution welcomed by the younger generation, who were soon saying that he had become a poet only in middle life.

One of the results of this change in direction is the amazing discrepancy between the attitude to women in the earlier and the later work. Indeed if we would see the lover in relation to social manners through the eyes of three different centuries, the eighteenth, the nineteenth and the twentieth, we might almost take as archetypes Goethe, Hugo and the later Yeats. Yeats wrote poems which neither Goethe or Hugo would have dreamed of publishing. Goethe remained the romantic lover even into old age. He has the sentiment of the German race and a keen awareness of woman's intrinsic charm. His attitude to woman never changes: it always included deference, humour and a keen appreciation of her varied appeal. At twenty he writes to Friederike in just the same way that he wrote to Ulrike von Levetzow half a century later. He is susceptible, playful, delightful in his letters; the perfect lover from one point of view, simply because he is so responsive, not merely to youth and sensual appeal—a weapon woman a little deprecates, because, although she knows its potency, she knows also that she shares it with so many others—but also to the indefinable charm of a particular individual. In Hugo pre-marital chastity and marital fidelity give way presently to the epic devotion to Juliette Drouet, but also to a succession of sordid intrigues with maidservants and others. He becomes an unpleasant old man. But even when, in old age, he seduces the lovely young laundress at Hauteville House, who from the first has been warned against him, he manages to convince her that her lover is a poet and not merely an elderly lecher, and he is able to command the girl's genuine

123

affection. He has lost his sense of human responsibility; the flesh has triumphed over the ecstatic declarations of his idealistic youth, but to the very end Hugo continues to write of love as a spiritual activity, and he would have been profoundly shocked by Yeats's down-to-earth outspokenness and his occasional phallic allusions.

Yeats was no Cuchulain to die fighting against the oncoming waves of disillusioned modernism. He had this horror of being left behind by his age, and he has said things in his later verse which it is inconceivable that either Wordsworth or Browning would have put into print, or that he himself could have written as a young man. He has renegued on the magnificent romantic rhetoric of his youth. Had his love been returned then, it might have been different. "I might have thrown poor words away and been content to live."

In *Hail and Farewell*, after the discussion on the sources of Yeats's inspiration, George Moore continues:

And from that day onwards I continued to meditate the main secret of Yeats's life, until one day we happened to meet at Broadstone Station. We were going to the West; we breakfasted together in the train, and after breakfast the conversation took many turns, and we talked of her whom he had loved always, the passionate ideal of his life, and why this ideal had never become a reality to him as Mathilde had become to Richard. Was it really so? was my pressing question, and he answered me: "I was very young at the time and was satisfied with . . .' My memory fails me, or perhaps the phrase was never finished. The words I supply, "the spirit of sense," are merely conjectural.

Of course some private psychological drama lay behind the contradictions in Yeats's character, and at least partly explained the various reversals of direction. Maud Gonne, the attachment to Mrs Shakespear, all those obscure ramifications of sexual preoccupation which undoubtedly go back into early childhood, yet may retain some of their force into old age, had each their influence. The vague dreams of youth were succeeded by the outspoken earthiness of the later verses, but the poet has hidden from us all that might explain his progress from one to the other.

That astute analyser of every aspect and inflexion of human character, Amiel, has certain self-observed and relevant comments to make on men as they grow older. He writes:

A loving woman is the thing best fitted to save us from the obsessions of lust and the torments of corrupting images. It is love that saves us from eroticism, and tenderness that exorcises the succubi. . . . Artistic prurience is a disgrace to middle age. When the hair begins to turn grey, wisdom is absolutely indispensable, for wanton ribaldry then becomes shocking and absurd. Is there anything more wretched than an old man with a licentious imagination and erotic tastes? He is repugnant to even the loosest of women. I have known some instructive and terrifying specimens. Sensuality of the imagination is also a debauch . . . Of all the various temptations that have assailed me since I have been of age to reflect, the only one to which I have frequently succumbed has been the taste for forbidden fruit, and the attraction of loose voluptuous reading.

Love and sensuality are mysteries and not jests. Ribaldry is the symptom of the maladjusted. Although he boasts of exploiting lust in the service of his Muse, Yeats does not confuse soul and body. Quite early he had written in Queen Emer's song:

> All love-longing is but drouth
> For the things come after death.

And his "Woman Young and Old" is quite clear upon the point:

> Flinging from his arms I laughed
> To think his passion such
> He fancied that I gave a soul
> Did but our bodies touch,
> And laughed upon his breast to think
> Beast gave beast as much.

125

It is not likely that we shall ever know much more of what Moore terms "the main secret of Yeats's life," although it is possible that the publication of his journal or of hitherto unpublished letters might throw light upon it. In his "A Man Young and Old" he begins by telling what we can interpret easily enough:

> She walked awhile and blushed awhile
> And on my pathway stood
> Until I thought her body bore
> A heart of flesh and blood.
>
> But since I laid a hand thereon
> And found a heart of stone
> I have attempted many things
> And not a thing is done . . .
>
> Maundering here, and maundering there,
> Emptier of thought
> Than the heavenly circuit of its stars
> When the moon sails out.

That is clearly Maud Gonne, and the second poem of the sequence reveals his own suffering:

> So like a bit of stone I lie
> Under a broken tree.
> I could recover if I shrieked
> My heart's agony
> To passing bird, but I am dumb
> From human dignity.

In "The Mermaid" he makes discovery of the flesh:

> Pressed her body to his body,
> Laughed; and plunging down
> Forgot in cruel happiness
> That even lovers drown.

But, after that, the poem-sequence becomes so cryptic that one is forced to agree with Strong that Yeats has covered up his tracks with all the cunning of an old fox.

126

Nevertheless all the coverts are worth drawing. One possessed the masterpieces. But that made it all the more frustrating to be baffled and mystified by the man. He had written lines like no other lines in the whole English language, and one felt outraged at feeling a sense of alienation and disapproval in his presence, but that was what happened. He seemed to hate all the milder virtues, and he could not keep this hatred to himself. It would transpire from time to time. He was the Arch-Poet, and, because he was the Arch-Poet, this absence of gentleness and this impatient pride became all the more distressing to me in the light of my naïve initial reverence. He was inhuman in that he seemed to have deliberately shed so many normal human traits. For example, it gave you a sense of surprise if he remembered your name or extended a hand when you were leaving, whereas A. E.'s abrupt, shy handshake on the doorstep of 17 Rathgar Avenue was part of the evening's ritual.

I irritated Yeats nearly always. I irritated him most when I was least anxious to do so. This applies especially to our later meetings, rather than to the ones already described; but even then the reservations in my hero-worship existed. A malevolent little elf seemed to arrange specially that he should always say something to incur my dissent. As for myself, I would say many things, platitudinous, ardent and probably absurd, to madden him. Exuberance, impulsiveness, a painstaking seriousness, a belief that if ideas are true they will fit themselves eventually into some lucid and logical arrangement, were the last things to win his favour. It infuriated him when I tried to press an idea to its ultimate conclusion, or when I anticipated or tried to indicate where his own idea was leading him; and he annoyed me by his apparent refusal to admit that ideas have any relation to one another, or form part of a logical whole.

Yeats was not a mystic. The mystic believes that there
127

is some complete pattern, some Whole into which all the parts fit, some Way which is worth seeking for its own sake. Yeats's mind moved, rather, amid isolated phantasmagorias, or at least in the same way that the mind moves in sleep, with sudden intense perception emerging from a background of vague cloud. It was intentionally undisciplined. To him poetic intuition was the substitute for philosophic analysis. But just as analysis can presently become entangled in itself and end in the driest of pedantry, so intuition can sail off into one aberration after another. Even where literature was concerned his thought was capricious. Strong writes:

Yeats was a fine example of the unscientific critic, by which is meant the critic who, instead of detaching himself impartially from what he is to inspect, illumines it by surrender to his own prepossessions. No man had a better eye for what was germane to or repugnant from his own thought. Where he was sympathetic, Yeats's criticism is unsurpassed. He had flashes of insight which put him among the masters. But, once off his own lines, he was increasingly uncertain, rejecting whole masses of work which did not interest him, forcing play or poem or novel to his own angle, and exaggerating much for the sake of a little which seemed to chime with his own mind. These prejudices were not conscious.

It is Strong also who points out Yeats's debt to Wilde for having remarked that a man could not speak the truth until he wore a mask. "He had Yeats's instant and fullest attention." Yeats in *The Trembling of the Veil* gives us some interesting glimpses of Wilde, without penetrating very deeply into his character, and he retails one, probably apocryphal, anecdote about Wilde in Dieppe after his release from prison, in a tone of singular brutality. We have come to associate the theory of the mask so much with Yeats that it would be curious if he really owed the theory originally to Wilde. It had certainly become an integral part of his nature, and contributed largely to the feeling of

128

strangeness which his presence induced. Everything he did or said was not necessarily studied, but it was pitched in a different key from other people's. By the time the situation had been dramatised by him, by the time the valid emotion had become part of the mask, and been projected, it had ceased to be itself and was something slightly different. Yeats's intellectual passions seemed separate from those of other men, in that they had become hierarchical and part of the ritual of his life. He had the authority of genius; but with it was the mannered arrogance of someone out of Pirandello's *Henry IV*. When the poet denounced the Englishman abroad, you felt that the Empire was about to fall into pieces. On the other hand, when he denounced Paudeen, who was his own nationality, you felt that Paudeen was too clever for him. He would ignore what Yeats wrote about him completely, he would continue to fumble at the greasy till, and neither Yeats's eloquence nor his rage could ever pierce the impenetrable hide of the gombeen-man and his like. The Irish are past-masters in the art of subtle denigration; a word, a phrase, a light-hearted jest, a sneer, but they have also learnt from experience the best mode of defence, which is to lie low and appear oblivious of the attack. The people in Ireland that Yeats attacked in his verse remained unperturbed, since they took care never to read him.

XV

I RETURNED to Switzerland in September. A long winter followed, with snow from October to May. I would read the *Irish Statesman* in a rickety armchair in my room at the top of L'Ecole Anglaise, pleasantly fatigued after an afternoon spent skiing with the children. Dublin was far away, and Yeats, and my other literary contacts, but thanks to this weekly journal I still felt a part of it all.

My first book had gone to W. B. and, if I had not been so tetchy, I might have heard his opinion of it. My second, which was a de luxe affair, printed in Paris by Ducros and Colas for the Greyhound Press, and with *pochoir*, i.e. hand-stencilled, watercolour illustrations by Charles Picart Le Doux, reached him only indirectly. Perhaps I forgot him; or perhaps there was some difference of opinion with Alister Mathews about presentation copies. I submitted the volume, however, in the literary contest of the revived Tailteann Games. This was the second time they had been held since Ireland's liberation, and it was hoped that they would be held indefinitely, at four-year intervals. It was a hope not to be fulfilled. Meeting the poet Fred Higgins in Nassau Street one day, when I returned again to Ireland the following summer, I learnt from him, unofficially, that my book had tied with Gogarty's for the Gold Medal in poetry. "The judges can't decide between them, and so the final decision has been referred to Yeats. Don't tell anyone. This is of course private."

As Gogarty had been given the Gold Medal already, at the previous games four years before, there was a hope that

I might be lucky and that they would give it to the younger man. But the hope was to be disappointed; history repeated itself and Gogarty received the Gold Medal. I was given the Silver. Simone Téry wrote an amusing account of the prize-giving in Iveagh Gardens, with the poets and athletes standing together in torrents of rain under the dripping trees. What I myself remember is being greeted by a top-hatted, morning-coated, grey-waistcoated Gogarty who, with—it seemed to me—typical Gogartian guile, shook me by the hand and remarked with pursed lips, "Ah, yes, you got something in the Dramatic Section, didn't you?"

My third book, *For Daws to Peck At*, was published by Gollancz about a year later. I must have sent a copy to Yeats but I do not appear to have given him an address, for his letter to me is addressed c/o the publisher.

April 25 [1929]   Via Americhe 12—8
                                                      Rapallo,
                                                         Italy
Dear Monck [*sic*] Gibbon
  Thank you for your book. I have read it and like its accurate speech and careful music.
  You have found your voice, and the words and emotion will deepen with life and study, and if both bring you to some tragic situation, or exultation, you will have all a poet needs.
  I am on my way back to Ireland but shall spend ten days or so in London.
                                               Yours ever
                                               W B Yeats.

It was kindly of him to say this. Actually life and the war had introduced me already to a number of tragic situations, and I had known exultation in Jersey, and its devastating aftermath. There was no need to prescribe either. I had known the intensity of both delight and despair.

Still, it was flattering to have had a letter from the great

131

man. I did not really expect Yeats to approve my poetry. Indeed it seemed to me that he must be the first person to detect in it a certain starkness, a certain poverty, compared to his own richness of imagery and phrase. I had at this time a firm belief that poetic quality is a matter of intensity of feeling, that inspiration is everything, and that the particular mode of expression—simple or complex—is a subsidiary matter.

If Yeats had dismissed my work as utterly worthless I would not have resented it, but would have been disposed, in certain moods, secretly to agree with him. As it was, his letter encouraged me, just as the long, detailed letters I had had earlier from A. E. had encouraged me greatly.

For Daws to Peck At was well received, and it was to be given a piece of fortuitous publicity of the sort that poets need so badly. Generally this takes the form of death; but occasionally some lesser intervention of providence is equally effective.

I had sent a copy of my book to a man whom I greatly admired, J. W. Mackail, former Professor of Poetry at Oxford. He wrote that he had read the poems with "high appreciation and unusual pleasure. I congratulate you not on promise, which is precarious, but on performance, which is certain." Quite unknown to me, Mackail passed the book to Baldwin, who was his cousin, and the Prime Minister quoted from it at some luncheon to journalists and the press. That good-natured and enterprising individual Victor Gollancz, who had risked publication, saw his chance and the public were soon being told that I was another Baldwin discovery, like Mary Webb. A stranger, Alan Steele, in the bookselling business, made himself equally helpful; and, within a few weeks, Gollancz was announcing a second edition, as well as a limited signed edition on hand-made paper with a vellum back, for those who could afford such a luxury.

Lily Yeats was among the friends to offer congratulations:

132

My dear Willy Monk,

Your fame is made and I hope you become at once a "best-seller" and that you and Winifred both vote for Baldwin's party.

I like your book enormously and we have two copies in the house—one very kindly given by your father and one bought by Elizabeth—and I am going to get a copy for my cousin Ruth Lane-Poole in Australia . . .

W. B. is to be back in England next week, and on here the week after. Mrs W. B. comes to Dublin next week, leaving him in London for a while—both very glad to get back. Rapallo was cold and influenza got the three people they knew.

Do you come over this year? I hope so. Respects to Winifred.

Your affectionate cousin
Lily Yeats.

I had married the previous year and was now settled in Dorset, but visits to Ireland were fairly frequent. In Swanage in the course of the next few years we encountered a number of friendly and interesting people, Archie Russell, Lancaster Herald, an authority on Blake and a great collector and connoisseur; Paul Nash and his wife; the singers Norman Nottley and David Bryndley, the dancers Hilda and Mary Spencer Watson, Jan and Cora Gordon and— soon to be a close friend—the composer Christopher Le Fleming. The latter had made fine settings to poems by Hardy and William Barnes and a superb setting for Yeats's "To an Isle in the Water," perfectly attuned to the mood of the little poem, and highly memorable. He told us that he had written repeatedly to the poet to ask for permission to publish it, but could get no answer. In the end I think he had taken French leave. I was to make his peace with the great man by sending it to him.

That explains this letter:

July 30 [1931]   Coole Park, Gort, Co. Galway

Dear Monck [sic] Gibbon

My wife looks after musicians for me. I have no ear—don't

know one tune from another. I cannot make head or tail of anything but little folk songs to which [I] listen as if they were something said. Music impresses me but I can no more judge of its quality than I can of the qualities of thunder or the sound of wind. So what is my praise worth?

Come in some Tuesday evening but phone first and find out if I am in town. Tuesdays not Mondays now.

Yours ever
W B Yeats.

XVI

I WAS to receive two letters of much greater interest from him the following March. A book by Robert Graves had sent me in search of the poetry of Gerard Manley Hopkins a few months before the general hue and cry began. We took the poems to Donegal with us, and, reading them where the pale-grey granite rock sloped, from amidst the heather, down to some tiny gravelly beach on the margin of a lake, we were soon converted. I was not interested in Hopkins's theories. Stresses are inevitable in the structure of a language, but they are partly also the imposition of the individual ear. And if the ear justifies a line, a mathematical count seems to me almost beside the point. What did interest me was Hopkins's resurrection of a poetic form that I imagined had become moribund. This was the sonnet. As a schoolboy I had loved sonnets and had accepted the fact that a contemporary sonnet must always seem a little tame. If a modern poet wrote a sonnet it was almost inevitable that it should suggest either Shakespeare or Milton or Wordsworth. Tennyson's brother wrote good sonnets, but of a rather luscious, mid-Victorian sort. Rossetti was excellent; but even at his best there is a suggestion of the literary exercise. Eventually I reached the conclusion that the sonnet was in certain respects dead; that it was useless to expect individual utterance in a sonnet. The form invariably took possession of the poet, rather than the poet of the form. Hopkins very quickly made me realise the folly of any such dogmatising. By injecting a little chaos into his sonnets he had instantly made the form alive once more.

I read him with delight, but quite without predatory design. He was very far from being up my street. When, however, I got back to Swanage in September, leaving my wife and small son behind for a few weeks with my parents, I found myself one night in my small room at the top of the Wolfeton Private Hotel, deliberately essaying a sonnet to Hopkins's memory in his own manner. There followed as a result two or three weeks of intense poetic activity. What Hopkins had done was to give me a sense of glorious liberty. The sonnets which I wrote varied from the multi-footed "Which o'erleaps itself" to the relatively orthodox "And Come Again to Carthage" which can be found in Robert Lynd's anthology and of which Canon Peter Green has written in his book on aesthetics, *The Problem of Art*: "It 'infected' me, as Tolstoy would say, for it and several others of the seventeen sonnets haunted me for days."

These sonnets were to give my father the greatest pleasure of anything I had achieved hitherto. When, a few months later, *Seventeen Sonnets* appeared I acknowledged my debt to the Jesuit poet almost too naïvely in my dedication. This gave many of the critics a stick with which to belabour me. A shrewd poet will never acknowledge his sources or allow his devotees even to imagine that he has had any. His Muse must spring fully armed like Athene from the head of Zeus if she is to be respected. And so wise poets keep their mouths shut, just as the precocious eighteen-year-old author of a recent French best-seller listed—Raymond Mortimer points out—almost every classic French novelist from Balzac to Proust as amongst those who had influenced her profoundly, but was shrewd enough to omit the name of Colette whose influence seemed to him paramount.

A copy of my book went to W. B. and I received his comments presently.

Dear Mr Monk Gibbon

I imagine your *Seventeen Sonnets* have been some time on my table but your work is difficult and has a strange atmosphere. One has not always the freedom from preoccupations to breathe. You have gained greatly in intensity of diction from Gerard Hopkins but lost in naturalness. Gerard Hopkins, whom I knew, was an excitable man—unfitted to active life and his speech is always sedentary, the reverse of that of his friend Bridges, when Bridges was at his best. Gerard Hopkins never understood the variety of pace that constitutes natural utterance. I have no copy of Bridges at hand and remember nothing but "The glitter of pleasure and a dark tomb" but that is sufficient. It is first swift and then slow, and suggests a man speaking with emotion. Hopkins is the way out of life, Bridges is the way into life. You need not however bother about these things if you are strong enough to pass into the second stage of poetic development. Paul Valéry seems to have passed through it in its most extreme form. For twenty years he neither wrote nor read poetry; he was finding, through mathematics, convictions. The first stage gives one diction, then one has to so subdue the diction that the reader can say "here is a man deeply moved speaking words that come spontaneously to his tongue." In my experience literature is a life-long war against the sedentary element in speech. You are too difficult and this is the sedentary element. When I write I again and again say to myself "I am living in the Himalayas talking to pilgrims " or "I am in Iceland a thousand years ago but I am also myself talking to (not writing for) certain young Mayo lads who are going to fish and have little learning." Which means that I must be timeless and yet find modern symbols. If I were an Englishman I might substitute Birmingham workmen for Mayo lads or I might not. One plays whatever trick brings sympathy. Then again there is a sense in which nothing matters but subject matter. I think that both Dante and Milton and perhaps Shakespeare toiled through libraries of works with the conscious purpose of learning to think poetically, which is much the same as believing in some scheme of the world.

Again and again I find your speech admirable, powerful,

vivid, rhythmical but am upset because I do not find the man.
I want to say, "My God how this man hates" or "How this man
loves" or if I can't get this I want original sin. I would be moved
by Sonnet VIII for instance if I could believe that you were
really praying or seeking God. Study seventeenth-century
Gaelic poets. Hopkins believe[d] in nothing. Remember what
Heine said about an Englishman saying his prayers.

Yours ever
W B Yeats.

It is an interesting letter, full of the man, and he must
have gone to some trouble to write at so great length. Not
that I agreed with all of it. It is an exaggeration to speak
of Hopkins as the way out of life. Many of his poems seem
the way into the very core of sensory impression. Nor is
Bridges for one moment the way into life. A good deal of
his work smells far more of the lamp and the library than
that of Hopkins: he is a cold poet: only when—as in his
exquisite "Pater Filio"—he reveals his tenderness, do we
feel that he has conquered his instinct of reserve, and then
he does it along lines very similar to those of his Jesuit
friend. It is amusing to note that Hopkins's own theory
of poetic speech is very little different from that of Yeats.
He held, as Donald Davie reminds us, that the language of
poetry should be "the current language heightened," based
on the spoken language of the time. Yeats had something
of a hunch, I suspect, against Hopkins; he has pooh-
poohed him to me as a man of so delicate a conscience that
he could not sleep at night from worrying whether he had
awarded his university candidates in their exam a completely just mark. Hopkins deprecates *Mosada*, which had
been given him by Yeats's father, in a letter to Coventry
Patmore. Yeats can never have seen this letter. But
Hopkins had called on Yeats's father at the latter's request and it is possible that he showed insufficient appreciation of the gift. When he comes to discuss Hopkins's
poetry in his introduction to *The Oxford Book of Modern*

Verse, Yeats makes it plain that he is wholly allergic to it. There he writes:

I read Gerard Hopkins with great difficulty, I cannot keep my attention fixed for more than a few minutes; I suspect a bias born when I began to think. He is typical of his generation where most opposed to mine. His meaning is like some faint sound that strains the ear, comes out of words, passes to and fro between them, goes back into words, his manner a last development of poetical diction. My generation began that search for hard positive subject-matter, still a predominant purpose.

This is nonsense from a number of angles. If the Countess Cathleen or the hero and heroine of *The Shadowy Waters* are illustrative of the search of Yeats's generation for hard, positive subject-matter, one can only say that the search in its initial stages was singularly unsuccessful. But what is hard subject-matter, and what soft? Is Yeats's Wild Old Wicked Man of greater literary specific gravity than Hopkins's bugler boy? Is a line like:

> What shall I do for pretty girls
> Now my old bawd is dead?

positive subject-matter, and one like

Man's mounting spirit in his bone-house, mean house, dwells,

negative and abstract?

One cannot say that one theme is harder or softer than another, any more than one can say that the brothel is more realistic than the marriage bed. All one can say is that the brothel is a more promising topic in our age because it quickens interest, and arouses jaded curiosities; whereas an epithalamium suggests conventional virtue and general acceptance, themes repugnant to the emancipated.

But when he goes on in his letter to discuss the two stages of poetic development Yeats throws considerable light on his own personal problem and his letter is of intense interest. It is possible that they are alternating phases rather than

139

successive stages. A poet must feed his imagination, and he must have some idiom ready for it when it overflows into utterance. I should have thought that Yeats's second stage was perhaps really the first. "Waiting upon the god" comes before the achievement of technical mastery. It is useless for a young poet to evolve an elaborate poetic technique, a "diction," unless he is already poet enough to feel the strong urgency of speech. Yeats was such a poet, and his great problem in the days when Moore knew him was to "find a style." Indeed he overstressed it. In *Hail and Farewell* we read how it became the continual topic of his conversation, until his friends began to say that he had found a style, but had nothing to say in it. They were wrong. Many critics would affirm that all his best poetry was still to come. But as he grew older the problem of a theme became as acute for him as the problem of a style. At such times he may have envied Valéry his twenty years of mathematical retirement. In "The Circus Animals' Desertion" Yeats gives tragic expression to his dilemma.

> I sought a theme and sought for it in vain,
> I sought it daily for six weeks or so.
> Maybe at last, being but a broken man,
> I must be satisfied with my heart, although
> Winter and summer till old age began
> My circus animals were all on show,
> Those stilted boys, that burnished chariot,
> Lion and woman and the Lord knows what.

The poem moves slowly through four more verses to its grim conclusion:

> Those masterful images because complete
> Grew in pure mind, but out of what began?
> A mound of refuse or the sweepings of a street,
> Old kettles, old bottles, and a broken can,
> Old iron, old bones, old rags, that raving slut
> Who keeps the till. Now that my ladder's gone,
> I must lie down where all the ladders start,
> In the foul rag-and-bone shop of the heart.

The intensity that Yeats gives to every line of his poetry is partly the outcome of his own strongly original, deliberately idiosyncratic mind; and partly a result of his insistence not, as he thought, on living speech and popular speech, but on highly individual speech. People do not talk as Yeats does in a poem; only Yeats does. But he has made his every inflexion familiar to us, so that we hear a living voice, most certainly a living voice, but it is Yeats's living voice. As Strong rightly says, "Yeats's verse gave dignity to everything it touched, from the political ideal to the lonely word. He could take a worn adjective and make it live as if for the first time: he could take an idea current in men's gossip and make it a piece of his poem. The secret was that he never put into his verse anything which his imagination had not fully assimilated."

This is nearer the truth than any of Yeats's theories on what is or is not sedentary speech. His own life had, as Maud Gonne said, followed "a road of outer peace," and perhaps this partly accounted for his so much relishing images of vigour and violence. My own life had run quietly into troubled waters. I had gone to the war little more than a child, had suffered severely as a result and was to feel its effects for a number of years. Yeats could not be expected to know this, but his sisters did. So far from wanting to place on record my hates or my fears, I could bring myself to speak of them at all only in severely restrained and dispassionate terms. I could not release what I had been at so great pains to control; nor could I triumphantly exhibit evidence of original sin when the whole tenor of my days in Jersey had been determined by the effort to achieve serenity and balance. My Muse was tight-lipped. The sonnet to which Yeats alluded in his letter is a fair example. It poses the question of the human status. It hints at—while at the same time implicitly rejecting—man's automatism. But it does so calmly, without any trace of *saeva indignatio*:

See now, pull string, both arms are jerked up high,
In action quite grotesque, most wholly droll;
Both legs as well, same time, galvanic fly,
Galvanic cord being god-head in control:
Arm supplication, quite absurd, beguiled
Limp from the shoulder, swung surrender, sad;
Leg gaiety, involuntary, wild,
More than a little, when one watches, mad!

Cheapest of toys, what irony of mind
Minds me of self and others, fortune still
Less favoured, whom to, so much blunted, blind,
This all too circumstanc'd life cedes little will?
Mere sport of things, for this and this thing sole
Did God give—God have mercy—immortal soul?

Yeats is right. This is not personal speech. For one thing anguish has been disciplined into reticence. The sting of the poem lies chiefly in that "all too circumstanc'd life." Trivialities dominate us. We are at the mercy of events. The reproach is aimed more at ourselves than at the Creator. It is we who have allowed ourselves to become Jumping Jacks, and the resultant antics are pathetic and absurd. The only touch of commiseration is for those "still less favoured by fortune" who would have needed exceptional force of character to have dominated their destiny.

When I received the letter I re-read a number of times the sentence "if I could believe that you were really praying or seeking God." What did W. B. mean by that? Of course, in their context in the sonnet, the words are a mere rhetorical ejaculation. That is all they are intended to be. But had he divined a certain duality in my nature? Of course I prayed, prayed daily and found no difficulty at all in praying. Prayer was natural, and Mahommedans were the only sensible people who could pause and pray in mid-street, whereas I felt a certain sense of embarrassment when I knelt down in the public sleeping-saloon of the Irish mailboat, lest someone should come and find me. But at the same time, although my life in one sense was based on prayer, I was an intellectual sceptic. That is to say I did not feel the arguments of any religion or creed were watertight. Like Pascal I could see a flaw here, an inconsistency there. But unlike Pascal it did not worry me. The contradictions arise because frail humans are so insistent, they prefer to be told they are betting on a certainty, if they make a religious bet at all. Each creed has to be explicit. The great religious teachers themselves did not labour any of these points. Jesus did not go about saying "I am the son of a virgin." Asked about the hereafter he could be as vague as "In my Father's house are many mansions." Buddha was not afraid to say "I do not know." Religion is a shot in the dark, but an essential one. It predicates what every intelligent man must predicate, purpose and design in life. And since the part cannot be greater than the whole, it predicates Tao, it predicates God.

"I would be moved by Sonnet VIII for instance if I could believe that you were really praying or seeking God." How astute he was, if he really meant all that I thought he did. I remembered how I had stood in front of the fireplace in A. E.'s great room at the top of Plunkett House and had said to him, "Nothing else would matter to me if I could really believe firmly in the human soul." What I meant was that, until we can confidently make such an affirmation and feel it deeply in our being—as A. E. did then, and as I have come to do more and more as I grow older—we are mere spindrift before the storm. We are unaware of our own essential nature.

I must have replied to the letter and queried some part of it, for I find another letter to me:

March 25th [1932]   at Coole Park, Gort. Co. Galway.

Dear Monk Gibbon:
I have not time for more than a few words. "Life death does
143

end"* is sedentary because those words are neither in the order of thought nor the order of speech. They are a jumble nobody ever found except on a piece of paper. The drawing room is no more sedentary than Roaring Camp. My generation revolted against "poetical diction" and Hopkins was of the generation that elaborated it. He had it in one form, Swinburne in another. His whole life was a form of "poetic diction." He brought his faint theatrical Catholicism to Ireland where [it] is not relished by the sons of peasants and perhaps died of the shock. What Heine said was that a Frenchman cursing was more pleasing in the sight of God than an Englishman saying his prayers.

Yours ever
W B Yeats.

I am just off to Dublin and then London.

Yeats is not quite fair. If Hopkins's life was a form of poetic diction, the same could be said with even greater truth of W. B.'s own. And if the inversion "Life death does end and each day dies with sleep" is inexcusable, then a great many other lines in English poetry will have to go too, including Yeats's "poetry and music I have banished." In fact, as I have shown, Yeats did not revolt against poetic diction. He revolted in favour of a poetic diction which would be entirely his own. He was like those rebels who overthrow an existing aristocracy as showy, effete and tyrannous, and presently appear wearing a whole chestful of decorations themselves.

It is true that he was continually on his guard against unreality in speech, but

> Slim adolescence that a nymph has stripped,
> Peleus on Thetis stares.
> Her limbs are delicate as an eyelid

can hardly be called living speech. And by the time he came to choose the pieces for his anthology, three or four years later, Yeats had come to think slightly better of Hop-

* "Life death does end and each day dies with sleep." (Hopkins, *Poems*, third edition, p. 107.)

Dear Monk Gibbon: I have not time for
more than a few words. "Life death
does end" is sedentary because
these words are neither in the order of thought
nor in the order of speech. They are a jumble
of words even from excess — on a piece of
paper. The ~~drawing room~~ drawing room is less more
sedentary than Roaring Camp. My
generation revolted against 'poetical diction'
& Hopkins was of the generation that
elaborated it. He had it in one form
Swinburne a another — His whole life is in
a form of "feeble diction". He brought
his faint theatrical catholicism & Ireland
where it is most unreal & the sons of peasants &
perhaps died of the shock. What Heine said
was that a french man cursing was more
pleasing in the sight of God than an Englishman
saying his prayers. Yours W B Yeats

I am now of & Dublin & then London.   March 26

kins, or else the rising tide of the latter's devotees may have influenced him, for he gives him seven pages and as many poems in his anthology, including the fine and highly characteristic "The Leaden Echo and the Golden Echo."

XVII

THE *Irish Statesman* had come to an untimely end. A
severe review by Donal O'Sullivan, Clerk of the Senate,
of a collection of Irish folksongs had led to a libel action by
the husband and wife who had made the compilation. The
action dragged on, expert after expert offered evidence, until
both the paper and the prosecutors had almost reached
bankruptcy. This was early in 1930, and the last poem of mine
to appear in the paper was published a few weeks before the
end and was called "Yeats's Earlier Poems." It envisaged
a scene of holiday on one of those wide golden beaches to
be found in Sligo and Donegal; an encounter between swift-
running, foam-splashed children and their absent-minded
progenitor, who had almost forgotten that he had brought
them into the world:

> On sands untrodden,
> Barefoot to the tide,
> With smoke from sodden
> Bogs blown to sweetness on the causeway wide
> Towards islands low,
> Green islands low, surmised still more than seen,
> Fleet as the spray,
> As lonely as the scene,
> And mild-eyed as the moon that rises now;
> Too sure to slip
> They run exultant, then halt suddenly,
> Sobered by this grave stranger,
> Scenting danger,
> Some scorn of lip,
> Some slight impatience of the moving hand
> Tracing strange patterns on the soon-swept strand;

146

Till he
Stops absently,
Sees tresses salt with brine,
"Whose are these children?—They indeed are mine!"

The image of the tall poet, distrait, aloof, roused out of
his reverie and unable to recognise his own offspring, was
not meant as an unfriendly one. Lily Yeats balked at one
of my epithets, and said firmly to me, "You meant moon-
swept, of course, and not soon-swept." "Oh no, I meant
soon-swept." It had seemed to me that the tide would
come in, as it does inevitably with most occult systems,
and obliterate all Yeats's traceries of interlocking gyres and
the like, which we find in *A Vision*; whereas his long-haired
poetic children, with their hair streaming in the wind and
flecked with spume, were safe for years to come, even
though their parent might for the moment have forgotten
them.

Lily said no more but, if she objected to "soon-swept,"
it is possible that W. B. did also. He passed no comment on
the poem and may never have read it.

I note that about this time I contemplated getting Lolly
to print a book for me as a private venture outside the
legitimate Cuala series. She had already done this for Lyle
Donaghy. She writes:

You asked about a book—we charged Lyle Donaghy too
little—for a similar book again we will have to charge £28 (for
100 copies). Lyle Donaghy's book had four sheets, 16 pages—we
pay more in proportion for the binding of 100 than we do for our
larger editions.

Lolly was my patroness. I did not feel that she was under
any obligation to pay for my poems when she used them as
wall-cards. I was highly flattered to see them in print,
embellished by beautiful hand-coloured woodcuts, and I
suspected that it was for my sake that they were there,
that she wished to encourage her youthful cousin, and that

147

all this advice and these underlinings in her letters were so that I might play my cards wisely when it came to dealing with W. B.

Unfortunately, however, Lolly's advocacy with W. B. was a boomerang which was liable to come back and hit whoever used it rather sharply on the nose. About ten years later, when Sturge Moore came to stay with Archie Russell in Swanage and he and I began to exchange reminiscences of the Yeats family over the dinner-table, I was a little shocked when Sturge Moore told me of how W. B. had once said to him, "I have two sisters, one of them is an angel, the other one a demon." It was said in jest of course, but I was able to cap it with another story, that Lily had told me, of how W. B. had remarked to his wife as he left the house one morning, "I have to discuss some business affairs with Lolly. We've arranged to meet at the Shelbourne Hotel. Then we won't be able to shout at one another."

No one found it very easy to collaborate with W. B. He liked his own way, and Lolly, with a mind of her own, was not the person to bow consistently before someone else's judgment. She had enormous pride in him. Both sisters had. She was a little afraid of him. (Lily had no need to be.) And she was one of those people who, when they plan to be particularly tactful, are as likely as not to end up in a morass of tactlessness. All her advice to me in her letters was meant to be helpful, but one careless injudicious remark on Lolly's part might undo all the good that she hoped to do you by her elaborate plannings. For example when *For Daws to Peck At* came out and enjoyed some fortuitous success, Lolly (perhaps with the incident of the refused introduction still in mind) remarked to me cheerfully, "W. B. has often been wrong about people before now and admitted it in the end to me. It will be the same with you, you will see. He'll admit to me he was wrong." This was all right for my ears, but if she took the same line with

148

the great man, there was always the chance that—Lolly being Lolly—the only result would be for Pharaoh to harden his heart. In fact, as we have seen, W. B. was to acknowledge the book with a very kindly letter.

Lolly had a mind of her own. Lily had a mind of her own too. But she had also limitless tact. If I want to symbolise Lolly I think of a crested white cockatoo on a stand in the zoo aviary, letting forth periodically an emphatic squawk. But if I think of Lily, the image becomes that of a cat curled up in an armchair, purring softly and waiting with justifiable confidence to be gently scratched behind the ears. Nevertheless, though Lolly and W. B. might shout at one another, they were bound together by that basic loyalty which united the whole family. They might bicker over small things, but that was only superficial. Lolly might dread the periodic descents of W. B. on the press, just as she dreaded those of the accountant. But she was fully aware that the press had been founded as W. B.'s way of helping his sisters and he gave a good deal of time and trouble to its finances. The truth is that W. B. instinctively resented all opposition, and it was not in Lolly's nature to be eternally or even temporarily submissive. She had been a gallant fighter all her life and remained one to the end; she had supported her menfolk through all their struggles for recognition, and it was too much to ask of her that she should add a final crowning virtue of being a "yes-woman" whenever they opened their mouths.

We came over from Dorset in 1932 and spent August in Donegal, a habit which was to be continued for many years. Then, at the beginning of September, I moved down to Co. Dublin to stay with my parents at Dundrum. Lolly arranged with Mrs Yeats that I should pay a visit to W. B. in his new home, which was only about two and a half miles away, before going back to England. It is possible that she had a kindly and ulterior motive in doing this. The poet had just returned from Coole Park where he had been with A. E.

planning an Irish Academy of Letters. On 18 September 1933, Hone tells us, it was formally established and the circular letter signed by Shaw and Yeats, which had been sent to a number of writers, inviting them to become members, was read out at a meeting by Lennox Robinson, together with some of their replies. My visit must have been a week or so before that. Yeats by now had moved out to a small house in pleasant grounds on the far side of Rathfarnham. It was not far from where the Stella of *Hail and Farewell* had once lived, and George Moore must have often passed its avenue gate on his way to visit Stella, or on the historic occasion of his visit to the half-deserted and now wholly ruinous Mount Venus. After Rathfarnham village the road narrows, shut in by trees on either side and by the walls of a number of small country places, each with its gateway, perhaps its gate-lodge, and certainly its inevitable shrubbery and short avenue-drive. A railed acre or two of field in front, and there stood the suburban retreat of a hundred years ago, as typical of its age as the slick, sunlit, unshrubberied neatness of the more compressed suburbs of today.

> All his happier dreams came true—
> A small old house, wife, daughter, son,
> Grounds where plum and cabbage grew,
> Poets and Wits about him drew;
> *"What then?" sang Plato's ghost. "What then?"*

I smile when I read that fourth line now. I was one of the poets but I was certainly not one of the wits, unless nitwits are included in the category. I had ridden over on my bicycle full of good intentions, determined to curb my verbosity. But the evening was the most unfortunate of any that I had spent in W. B.'s company, and, so far from creating the good impression that I had wished, I did just the reverse.

Yeats was full of his plans for the new Academy. An entry in my journal reads:

I forget whether I had heard about it already. I may have done so from Higgins, who was there that night, and Yeats's manner gave me the impression, rightly or wrongly, that I was being weighed in the scales. Gogarty arrived and amused me. He had no sooner sat down than he remarked to Yeats that he would sooner be left out of it all, he did not want to be a member, he was a Catholic and for a Catholic there might be complications. "Leave me out, Yeats. Leave me out." This was the right approach to W. B. There was never anyone with whom Brer Rabbit's technique of "Don't throw me into the briar patch, Brer Fox" was more effective. He liked to arrange everything as though in a drama, or rather a melodrama, the more deviously the better. Indeed he did harm, I think, to the younger generation of writers in Ireland by his mysterious plotting and counterplotting over trifles. For whereas he and Synge and A. E. and Lady Gregory had been a friendly co-operation of enthusiasts, the younger generation who gravitated towards Yeats found themselves part of a detective story. I have listened to Higgins, telling me at enormous length how Yeats had plotted unsuccessfully to get a Blue Shirt ballad of his own sung at the Abbey Theatre while gulling him (Higgins) by the promise of having some of his ballads sung at the same time. It all seemed the most absurd storm in a semi-literary, semi-political teacup.

I may not then have known about the Academy beforehand, but I certainly had set out that evening resolved to be of good behaviour, for the very same page in my journal records:

I made my way to Riversdale about eight o'clock in my usual state of acute literary excitement . . . I also went full of good resolutions. Lolly had given me a hint that W. B. did not like to be argued with or contradicted. I did not really need it, for I knew it well already. But I was determined to bear it in mind.

Higgins was there, Gogarty was there, A. E. was there. I cannot remember anyone else. We sat round the fire in the front of the two adjoining sitting-rooms, a pleasant homely room with a dark, nondescript wallpaper. It had nothing in the manner of the high-ceilinged grace of the Merrion Square room, but rather, if anything, a touch of a

151

Jane Austen dower house. As usual, and despite all efforts to control them, I was no sooner settled in my armchair than my thoughts began to radiate out in good-will in the direction of A. E. while at the same time they manifested their usual alarming tendency to cross-examine W. B.

However, the evening began well, with Gogarty's plea for exclusion from the Academy, followed by a story from him about a stable laneway in Clyde Road which amused Yeats. George Moore's name was mentioned and instantly that favourite topic, was he or was he not impotent, and, if impotent, always impotent or only impotent on his own confession after forty, was once more being discussed. It looked as though Yeats was trying to use Gogarty as his stalking-horse, getting him to say things in print about Moore which he had not the courage to say himself. For a long time we had been told that certain passages in Yeats's autobiography could not be published until Moore was dead. Moore was my friend. He had made fun of Yeats in *Hail and Farewell*, but no more ill-naturedly than Max Beerbohm in his famous cartoon. True he put into print the remark of some Dublin *littérateur*, that Yeats had taken his Muse to London, put paint on her cheeks and sent her down Piccadilly, an accusation which no poet could be expected to tolerate. But the rest of Moore's portrait is merely humorous and not intended to hurt. Lily Yeats told me that she once found herself seated beside George Moore at a dinner party, a few years after *Hail and Farewell* had been published. He implied to her that he would be grateful if she could effect a reconciliation between himself and the poet; he had never intended to be offensive, it was all only meant in fun. Lily however had intimated her inability to assume the role of peacemaker in this particular quarrel. Moore had probably added to his crime in that he consistently ennobles A. E., despite the fact that he, Moore, has no real understanding whatever of the outlook of a mystic. A book, he would have said, must have light and shade,

152

someone had to be given an heroic role and A. E. was best qualified for it. As for Yeats, if a man looks like a folded umbrella, why should I be forbidden to say so?

The talk passed from Moore, and Moore's hypothetical impotence, to impotence in general and to the various writers suspected of it. Yeats told us with a snort of relish of someone who claimed authoritatively that Jane Carlyle had burst out laughing in Carlyle's face on their marriage night, so great was his ineptitude. I could have made my own interesting contribution to the symposium by revealing that J. P. O'Reilly had whispered to me one evening at Rathgar Avenue not so long before that he was quite sure that Yeats himself was now impotent. It was fashionable at this period to be preoccupied with the physiological and to attribute everything to a sexual cause. "But his two children are not so old," I had protested incredulously. O'Reilly however had pursed his lips and shaken his head. He seemed to think that impotency could descend upon a father suddenly, out of the blue. For all I know it can.

It may have been Carlyle's humiliation which—having focussed attention upon sex—made me say presently that I thought it in questionable taste for Aldous Huxley in *Time and Tide* to announce that homosexual relationships were greatly on the increase in England since they were more economical, safer and carried less responsibility. *Time and Tide* was owned by a woman and edited by a woman, and in the 1920's homosexuality was not yet the stock topic which it has since become. The tone of Huxley's remark—with its bland acceptance, if nothing else, of the economic factor in intimate human relationships—had seemed to me particularly unsuitable in such a paper. Yeats brushed the whole matter aside with lordly contempt. Homosexuality? The Greeks? "Simply a matter of birth control." This sweeping judgment was typical of him. It is impossible to believe that *all* homosexuality has arisen out of man's desire to protect himself against the consequences of the procreative act. If that is so we may expect its gradual disappearance in the course of the next few centuries. But it was part of Yeats's nature to abhor the critical examination of any question. He preferred always to produce his dictum and leave it at that.

This attitude may have derived from his father, although, as Hone once said to me, J. B. Yeats was an example of that very rare thing, a father influenced by a son. Nearly twenty years before this his father wrote in a letter to W. B.:

The chief thing to know and never forget is that art is dreamland and that the moment a poet meddles with ethics and the moral uplift or thinking scientifically, he leaves dreamland, loses all his music and ceases to be a poet. . . . A man with his wife or child and loving them, a man in grief and yielding to it, girls and boys dancing together, children at play—it is all dreams, dreams, dreams. . . . When the essential sap of life is arrested by anger or hatred we suddenly are aware of the actual, and music dies out of our hearts and voices—*the anger subtly present* in ethical thought—as it is also in most kinds of argument; how many poems has it laid low?

This is excellent poetic advice. Whatever of the poet is in me instantly subscribes to it; but a coexistent moralist qualifies the acceptance by refusing to believe that ethics can lie completely outside the scope of art. Plato is an artist and a moralist. So are hundreds of others. The Greek tragic poets are largely concerned with ethical issues; so—though in very much lesser degree—was Shakespeare. In fact the more closely one examines the stimulating dictum of the old artist the more necessary it becomes to limit and qualify it.

I kept silence. If W. B. liked to write off homosexuality as merely a measure of birth control, then he must be allowed to do so. I had had a similar if less provocative illustration of the method earlier in the evening. Before the other guests arrived I had been describing to Yeats a particularly vivid dream which I had had some months before.

154

I had seen in my dream a four-page art-folder. On the front page, in a coloured design rather like a Persian painting, was a wood with slender red stems of innumerable pines rising up a hillside one behind the other. I used to see just such a wood and just such an arrangement of pine-trunks on a certain ride which I took frequently on horseback from Swanage to Studland. But now, in this wood, diagonally across the page, from the top right-hand corner to the bottom left, ran an open glade, and at either end of this were two striking objects. At the top of the narrow glade was the torso of a horse with a heavily armoured rider seated upon it. I think that both horse and rider were headless, but what one noticed immediately was the enormously developed muscular strength of the animal, and the man's black-and-gold armour—like Persian armour or the lacquered armour of the Japanese—as well as the great bow which he carried. In the bottom left-hand corner, with its graceful head slightly turned to look upon the glade, was a snow-white deer.

In my dream I opened out the folder and found that the centre page was given to exactly the same scene, although double the size. But in this version the body of the headless warrior was half-turned in the saddle; he had fitted a golden arrow to the bow, and was drawing it back so far that he gave the impression of enormous strength. Halfway down the glade, with the naïveté of mediaeval art, another great golden arrow was speeding on its way, and at the bottom of the glade the white fawn had sunk to its knees, the arrow was piercing its shoulder, and blood was streaming from the wound.

I turned with interest to the last page of the four. There to my surprise I found a design in a completely different idiom from the others. The first two pictures had been in eastern or pseudo-eastern style. The warrior's armour had been jet-black like the horse, but patterned with a delicate design of gold traceries. The colours had been vivid greens and mellow tawny, but here the picture was modernist in conception and execution, similar to the hand-stencilled coloured illustrations which Charles Picart Le Doux had done for my book *The Branch of Hawthorn Tree*. Even in my dream this sudden change in mode of painting gave me a quick stab of astonishment, and I was still more surprised to find that the subject of the painting was not, as I had expected, the same wood for a third time, but a completely different scene, a small group of dilapidated buildings of uneven height, rather similar to the group in Le Doux's clever design to my poem "The House." Unlike them, however, the setting was incredibly sordid and depressing— and these wash-coloured tenements were surrounded by the scorched and blackened stumps of trees. The fawn had been slain; the wood was gone; and instead there was this savage scene of urban desolation, a wilderness of bricks and dustbins, with the charred stumps of the trees as a reminder of what once had been.

It did not need a Joseph at Pharaoh's court to interpret the parable. Even in my dream I was perfectly aware what its symbolism meant, and only amazed at the artist's boldness in switching so abruptly, yet so effectively, from the style of Persian miniatures to that of the French modernists. The white fawn was beauty; the horse and warrior were blind, relentless force; and it was appropriate that the arrow speeding on its way should be gold, for, in the modern world, it is the arrow of Mammon, the arrow of profit, that in the hands of overwhelming power—political or economic —insists that beauty must be slain. And the results, the drab and bedraggled squalor of those few roofs, the countless stumps where the green glade had once been; and that epitomised sense of desolation—it did not need waking intelligence to know that this symbolised our modern world, in which expediency decides all, and beauty goes down before influences too relentless for her to have any chance of escape.

It is curious how the mind draws from identifiable sources
—the wood and the rising succession of pine-trunks passed
on my rides to Studland, Le Doux's designs for *The Branch
of Hawthorn Tree*—but weaves them into a dramatic and
logical pattern. The great shoulders of the horse with their
ripples of muscle, the lifted knee as in some immense
equestrian bronze, the half-turned body of the warrior as
he drew back the bow to its extreme limit, achieved all that
was required, without any head, without any further dis-
traction of face or person; and then the abrupt transition
to the debris of our urban civilisation.

I had told my dream to W. B. because I knew that he
was interested in dreams and in symbolism. He was interested, but it was all summed up in an instant in a single
phrase, "Ah, to be sure, the Cretan Myth." This meant
nothing to me. I repeated "the Cretan Myth?" with only
the very slightest interrogative inflexion, so as not to annoy
him. "Yes, you'll find it all in my book." Which book,
what book, I cannot remember now—but it was there, he
said, and I had only to refer to it.

Lolly had issued her warning: W. B. did not like to be
contradicted or argued with. But my strictures upon
Aldous Huxley, or the tone and manner of them, had
already annoyed him. And now there took place an absurd
incident which should really have been completely without
significance, but which nevertheless served to fire a charge
of latent hostility, in my breast at any rate. I cannot remember what we were talking about. But I know that I
said that St Paul's comparison was too popular with the
occupants of pulpits, where he says that the resurrection
of man's body corresponds to the seed falling into the
ground. It is not really valid, because, of course, the true
analogy lies between the wheat's yield and man's progeny,
that is to say, he is reborn in his children. It was a legitimate comment, and far from pro-clerical: but Yeats used
it as an excuse to lean over towards me, fix me with his eagle

157

gaze and say in an almost savagely arch tone "You keep very *strange* company!" The devil I did. My father, the man I loved best in the world, was a clergyman. Yeats must know that. He had baptised one if not both of the poet's children. Why should he make this silly, offensive, and largely irrelevant remark? Was Archbishop Gregg, whom W. B. admired so much, slapping his thigh and saying to me once of the long controversy with Cardinal MacRory in the columns of the *Irish Times*, "He made hares of him!" strange company? Was old Dean Ovenden, wit and humorist and raconteur, a man John Butler Yeats would have relished, strange company? Was Father John Butler, who had gone to Gallipoli with the Irish regiments, and to whom the poet Winifred Letts had introduced me, strange company? Well, they were no stranger at any rate than some of Yeats's own company in the past; indeed, not nearly as strange as the Blavatskys, the MacGregor Mathers, and all those weird cliques against whom he had once been kind enough to warn me.

I said nothing. There was nothing to say. His remark was made with a sneer and was presumably intended to be flattening. It was plain that I had once more incurred his displeasure. If I had wanted confirmation of this it would have been given me when I rose to go, an hour or so later. At the door of the room he paused, handle in hand, and fixing me with a stern gaze said, apropos of nothing, "You live too much out of Ireland."

XVIII

THAT remark, considering what was happening on the literary front, had considerable significance. Indeed it may have been intended as a pronouncement *ex cathedra*. Yeats was already classifying the people he had in mind for his Academy. Hone, writing of the foundation of the Academy and of its division into members and associate members, says: "The work of 'Associates' was classified as 'less Irish' than that of full members. But the distinction caused some heart-burnings, and one of those invited to be an Associate [almost certainly Dunsany] remained convinced that Yeats elaborated the whole project in order to insult him."

The Academy, like most things in Ireland, got off to a highly controversial start. The letter of invitation to become founder members went out in the names of Shaw and Yeats. George Moore ignored it and James Joyce refused. Sean O'Casey publicly disclaimed all intention of giving it his support, while Douglas Hyde and Daniel Corkery held that an Irish Academy should consist of writers in Irish. Stephen MacKenna, the translator of Plotinus, was among the first Associates named but declined the invitation 'out of modesty' though supporting the institution. Gogarty, the bishop who had refused the mitre, was one of the seven foundation members of the original Council.

If one studies the letter of invitation now, it seems too narrow and controversial a document for the inauguration of such a body. It reads more like the manifesto of a caucus. If Yeats had been wise, he would have given his Academy a broader and more authoritative basis and included—as the French Academy does from time to time—some prominent Catholic scholar or even cleric. But according to Liam Brophy, Yeats "repudiated the Gael and . . . had a desperate anxiety to provide Ireland with an intellectual background distinct from that of England and also from that of Catholicism." The actual document has an almost political rather than literary flavour:

Dear Sir, [September 1932]

We have at present in Ireland no organization representing *Belles Lettres*, and consequently no means whereby we Irish authors can make known our views, nor any instrument by which action can be taken on our behalf.

There is in Ireland an official censorship possessing, and actively exercising, powers of suppression which may at any moment confine an Irish author to the British and American market, and thereby make it impossible for him to live by distinctive Irish literature.

As our votes are counted by dozens instead of by thousands and are therefore negligible, and as no election can ever turn on our grievances, our sole defence lies in the authority of our utterance. This, at least, is by no means negligible, for in Ireland there is still a deep-respect for intellectual and poetic quality. In so far as we represent that quality we can count on a consideration beyond all proportion to our numbers, but we cannot exercise our influence unless we have an organ through which we can address the public, or appeal collectively and unanimously to the Government.

We must therefore found an Academy of *Belles Lettres*. Will you give us your name as one of the founder members?

In making this claim upon you we have no authority or mandate beyond the fact that initiative has to be taken by somebody, and our age and the publicity which attaches to our names makes it easier for us than for younger writers.

Please send your reply to the Provisional Hon. Secretary, George Russell, Esq., 17 Rathgar Avenue, Dublin.

Yours faithfully,

G. Bernard Shaw

W. B. Yeats.

Soon after this had been sent out, Yeats went abroad. His health necessitated wintering in the south of France. A. E. was left to carry out a long defensive action, replying to the numerous letters attacking the new Academy which appeared in the columns of the *Irish Times*. He did so with spirit and eloquence.

Yeats had always been a controversialist, although he kept out of this particular controversy. His pugnacity had helped him to survive the initial rigours of his vocation. But in later life it seemed sometimes that he enjoyed throwing the apple of discord for its own sake. Some of his earlier dissensions—like the *Playboy* riot—were forced upon him, and there he showed courage and firmness. Others are explained by his own quick, impulsive temperament. He quarrelled, for example, with his benefactress Miss Horniman because of her indignation that the Abbey Theatre had not closed its doors like the other Dublin theatres for King Edward VII's death. In fact Yeats had been in France at the time, but he was soon drawn into the fracas and wrote to her: "I am amazed that you should have published such a letter without even waiting for Robinson's explanation and that, explanation or no explanation, you should have done so much injury to a movement you have helped and cared for."

His early quarrel with A. E., which led to a nine-year gap in their correspondence, was the result of Yeats's high-handed insistence that A. E. should break his word to Digges and withdraw the permission which he had given him to perform his (A. E.'s) *Deirdre* in America. Sooner than go back on his word A. E. preferred to resign his post as Vice-President of the Theatre Society. This, in 1904, was not their first disagreement. In 1900 A. E. had, as we have seen, written to him "I find nothing to agree with in your letter and see clearly that in mysticism and in our ideas we have little or nothing in common. Of course that is desirable enough, as uniformity is detestable, but you see that I must follow the law of my own being and do my work in the way I have hitherto found it possible to get any inspiration. If I held your ideas I could never write another line."

A. E.'s protégés were always anathema to W. B. George Moore in *Hail and Farewell* tells of Yeats's sneer, "I hear that Dunsany is going to found a literary review to give groundsel to A. E.'s canaries." They were not always even canaries, they could sink lower in the natural scale. In *The Green Helmet*, which was published in 1910, one meets for the first time the tone of angry mockery in the poetry. Immediately following a not very effective epigram lashing out against the students of the National University for joining in a campaign against immoral literature, comes another "To a Poet [A. E.], who would have me Praise certain Bad Poets, Imitators of His and Mine."

> You say, as I have often given tongue
> In praise of what another's said or sung,
> 'Twere politic to do the like by these;
> But was there ever dog that praised his fleas?

Fleas or canaries—literary ornithologists and entomologists must decide the question for themselves—there were reprisals. One of the poets against whom he was supposed to have directed his four lines of venom struck back. Yeats had driven to political meetings on an outside-car with Maud Gonne and his fervour had been sincere enough. But by the time *The Green Helmet* was published he was the darling of the London drawing-rooms.

To a Poet

> I too, with Ireland, loved you long ago
> Because you sang, as none but you could sing
> The cause we held the dearest; now I know
> How vain your love was and how mean a thing.
>
> And not to you whose heart went anywhere
> Her sorrows's holy heritage belongs.
> You could have made of any other air
> The little careful mouthful of your songs.

This is dignified and fierce, and in some measure justified. Yeats's patriotism was not assumed; but it was his songs that mattered. Seamas MacCall once said of him, "He rifled the Irish pantheon to build himself a rockery." As he grew older it was the Anglo-Irish, his own class, that interested him, rather than the Celts of the heroic age. Liam Brophy writes with extreme bitterness:

> Yeats's childishness was apparent in his repudiation of the past which had given him his finest inspiration. That came in 1911 when he published a bitter poem on his former ideals. Had he submitted to the beneficent influence of Dr Douglas Hyde and Lady Gregory he would have learnt to know the true Ireland and continued to write poetry of authentic white magic; he might even have come to understand the real soul of Ireland. But he went after black magic, spurned the popular cause and denounced patriotism. He tried to eliminate the marks of his race from his former poems, and told how he cast off his singing robes embroidered with the old mythologies, "for there's more enterprise in walking naked." And having repudiated the Gael he attached himself with pathetic fervour to the Ascendancy. In 1933 he wrote: "Berkeley, Swift, Burke, Grattan, Augusta Gregory, Synge, Kevin O'Higgins (a Catholic in fact) are the true Irish people and there is nothing too hard for such as these."

Between literary quarrels, political quarrels and religious and philosophic quarrels there was plenty to feed his contentiousness. It was partly his own choice; partly imposed on him:

> Much did I rage when young,
> Being by the world oppressed.

But long after the world had ceased to oppress him—the oppression of neglect, perhaps the keenest of all those felt by poets—it was still his wish to

> seem, though I die old,
> A foolish, passionate man.

Dame Ninette de Valois has recently told us of his quarrel with Edmund Dulac:

I can remember a certain turmoil between Yeats and Dulac and the shock it was to the decorum of the B.B.C.; the eventual disentanglement was the result of months of feminine underground movement on the part of two devoted wives, brightly aware of male childishness. Yeats had been once more trying to broadcast an example of Irish poetry set to music by Dulac . . . the poet was upset over the English rendering of the songs, Dulac elated. Yeats expounded how such a rendering would make it impossible to face his Dublin friends again, so ashamed he was at the let-down to them all. The musical but fiery Frenchman, with quite different views as to who must not be let down, informed Yeats that he must, if necessary, offend Dublin, as he happened for the moment to be in a civilised country. The dignified pale young men of the B.B.C. went several shades paler and Yeats stalked out. The broadcast was highly successful; two wives worked in mutual accord for several months to heal the wound inflicted.

An even stranger story is that of his behaviour to Bodkin. Hone tells it:

One afternoon he came unexpectedly to Bodkin's house and suddenly said, "I have for a long time entertained and spread prejudices against you, which I have lately felt to be quite unfounded. With your consent I will go to certain members of the Government and explain my altered views." Needless to say, Bodkin hastily dissuaded him from putting this quaint but generous impulse into effect.

I demur to the word generous. Courageous would be a better one. It is a little less than generous to say that you have been wronging a man for years in your conversation and now propose to do what you can about it. I know a little of the inside of the quarrel, for, a number of years before, on one of my visits to Lily Yeats she had remarked to me: "W. B. has had a perfectly terrible letter from Bodkin." It was at the time of the election of Lucius O'Callaghan as Director of the National Gallery of Ireland. Yeats may not have been too scrupulous in his opposition

164

to Bodkin's candidature, and, when the election was over, Bodkin had blown off steam, quite a lot of steam. When O'Callaghan resigned, Yeats again opposed Bodkin with another candidate (the present holder of the post), Chevalier Thomas McGreevy. In fact it was only after Bodkin was elected that Yeats, a regular attendant at the meetings of the Governors, offered his olive branch.

That is equally characteristic. Yeats never realised that, if you have been unfair to a person, it is not enough to raise a hierarchical hand, murmur a brief recantation, and expect all to be immediately well. Furthermore, he lays himself open to the not very pleasant suspicion of modifying his standpoint only after those whom he had wronged had shown a sufficiently formidable resistance. *Vae Victis.* A Bodkin who had not succeeded to the directorship might easily have enjoyed Yeats's dislike and contempt to the end of his days. I do not suggest that this line of conduct was conscious. But certainly when W. B. could not override opposition his natural impulse was to make one last effort to get his own way by turning the enemy's flank, even if this meant subduing a strong former animosity. Dunsany, for example, reacted so sharply to associate membership of the Academy that he was presently made a full member, and in 1933 was given the Harmsworth Prize. Having insulted Alfred Noyes, despite Dorothy Wellesley's pleas that he should first make more sure of his facts, Yeats republished his Casement poem with the offending line removed and referred to Noyes's "noble letter;" but these gestures came a little late; he had gravely traduced a fellow-poet without waiting to verify his charges.

As a controversialist he was hasty and ill-considered. In his youth he had quarrelled with his political associates in much the same fashion. I see from my journal that he once remarked to me: "Excitability is not strength. The excitable man is not the strong man." But in fact he frequently allowed excitability to get the better of him.

There is little doubt that he was not at his best in a quarrel. I shall not libel the opposite sex by saying that when he quarrelled he employed the tactics of a woman. Women, to give them their due, quarrel just as openly as men, and are often considerably less spiteful. Yeats quarrelled with the relentless deviousness of a eunuch of the Sultan. Strong is right when he says that he was proud of his cunning.* He hated opposition, and, if he could not overcome it directly by a display of superior force, he might reverse his tactics and try the effect of a display of clemency. It was not malevolence, I believe, which made him aggressive. It was partly that general contentiousness which he had revealed even in the nursery, and, still more, that craving for the dramatisation of life which—to transfer to himself the simile he accorded Maud Gonne—made him one who

> lived as 'twere a king
> That packed his marriage day
> With banneret and pennon,
> Trumpet and kettledrum,
> And the outrageous cannon.

Some of those on whom the cannon was turned had every reason to think it outrageous. Their real crime was that they had never kissed the rod, they had never made that act of general submission which Roman potentates and mediaeval seigneurs exacted from friend and foe alike. Yeats could not brook opposition. His relations with the poet Seumas O'Sullivan are a typical case in point. O'Sullivan was one of A. E.'s most ardent disciples and had very early come under Yeats's displeasure. He was the poet who had shown fight in "the little careful mouthful

* "He was exceedingly effective in the world of affairs, and proud of his cunning. His sense of reality, the shrewdness he possessed in high degree, showed him times out of number how to manage a man or a situation, and the temptation to turn aside was often irresistible. A feeling for mischief aided it. 'I must smooth him down,' he said softly, when a lifetime friend had gone off in a huff. 'I must smooth him down.' His eyes gleamed behind their glasses, his lips moved silently: and the means adopted, a quite unnecessary display of virtuosity, were brilliantly successful."

of your songs." Yeats evidently decided it was time bygones should be bygones. O'Sullivan was a respected figure in the Dublin literary world, editor of that highly valued quarterly, the *Dublin Magazine*, and a poet and essayist of considerable distinction. And so Seumas was made not merely a full member of the Academy but one of the seven foundation members first announced and a member of its Council.

The olive branch had been extended. But Yeats had not secured the fief he had hoped for. As with Dunsany, there were too great temperamental differences—or possibly similarities. Seumas—just as contentious as Yeats in his own way—was never cut out for the part of yes-man in Council meetings. In a very short time Yeats was doing his best to rid himself of this difficult customer; was striking the table pontifically with his hand and exclaiming, "We must have a unanimous Council"; and presently Seumas was off the Council and peace presumably reigned once more.

My journal records that in one of my meetings in London with Harold Macmillan when I was working on *The Living Torch* he remarked to me: "I don't attempt to keep pace with the quarrels of my Irish authors. They are bosom friends when I meet them on one occasion; a few months later the same people are deadly enemies. I keep outside it all."

He showed his good sense. Writers of any nationality can be quarrelsome. The friendships and subsequent quarrels and still more subsequent revived friendships of Sainte-Beuve rival anything the Irish could possibly produce in that way. But to some extent Yeats—in my opinion—fostered this trait. In his youth he had been all too well aware of the value of cohesion. He and his friends practised a reciprocity which almost amounted to log-rolling, as every generation of younger writers does, drawn together by the exigencies of their campaign against the unfriendly world. Later Yeats had shown great loyalty to Lady Gregory and to Synge. We are told that Synge maintained his reserve

167

where Yeats was concerned, but he must have been fully aware of his debt to the poet. It was only when it came to his dealings with the younger generation that Yeats seemed to sow dragon's teeth; whereas A. E. was a unifying force, absolutely determined to ignore all vendettas and to dissolve all animosities under the rays of his benevolent gaze at Rathgar Avenue. Indeed, part of the explanation of W. B.'s propensity for throwing the apple of discord or—if that is an exaggeration—for establishing situations full of tension and very closely resembling a war of nerves, was probably that A. E. was this centre of calm, this point round which opposites could circle and even presently coalesce.

Of all the younger writers in Yeats's circle the one to establish closest contact with him was the poet F. R. Higgins. He lived a couple of miles from Riversdale on the far side of Rathfarnham, in a small house on the banks of the Dodder. A contemporary, somewhat given to irony, once said to me: "Fred collects a little whitewash from every wall he leans up against," but actually Higgins's talent was individual and no-one can doubt its authenticity for a moment who reads his fine poem on his father, or the one on Padraic O'Conaire. Higgins believed in the value of literary intercourse and was at one time the *fidus Achates* of Austin Clarke, who was striving to bring back into contemporary Irish verse not only the use of assonance but certain of the free native rhythms derived from Gaelic sources. When that friendship presently went the way of so many literary friendships, Higgins, who died at the early age of forty-four, was for a time without literary coadjutor. But in the closing years of his life, probably after Yeats had moved to Rathfarnham, he became the latter's faithful associate, and was made a director of the Abbey Theatre and Secretary of the Academy.

Higgins had far too much independence to be exploited by anybody. As we have seen, in a letter to Dorothy Wellesley, Yeats says that Higgins is keeping out of his way, being afraid to meet him because he had given a vote at the Academy of which he (W. B.) disapproved. Higgins had plenty of sly humour and a fair measure of adaptability, and I think that the friendship with Yeats was cemented because Yeats was able to imagine that he was managing Higgins, and Higgins was able to feel that he had retained his independence, each with about the same measure of actual truth. Higgins certainly prided himself on being able to stand up to Yeats and on refusing to be bullied by him. Nevertheless the friendship flourished because fundamentally they suited one another. Indeed it would be almost possible to contend that the racy bawdiness of Yeats's later poetry derived from Higgins. He came from Protestant farming stock in Meath, had a charming little wife who was devoted to him and to whom he was devoted. But he liked to pose as a consumer of numerous malt-balls in countless bars, just as he liked to employ the bluntest down-to-earth phraseology in his later poetry, in contrast to the lyric lightness of his earlier. After a time some of Yeats's personal mannerisms seemed to take root in the younger man.

Soon Higgins was involved in a number of Yeats's activities. He was my friend, and rumour was already afloat that Yeats had been asked to do an Oxford anthology which would be the making or the marring of us all. But Higgins, when asked to bear me in mind, and, if a right moment arrived, to remind W. B. tactfully of my existence, explained that he had nothing whatever to do with the project and was quite without influence. "What I can do— because I am co-editor with him—is to include you in the new series of Broadsides." This Cuala activity had been revived in a slightly larger and more delightful form than ever. Higgins chose a poem from my book which we both thought suitable. But it was not destined to appear. When I next saw him he had to explain to me that W. B. had rejected it. It was not Irish enough. I was not Irish enough. W. B. had overruled his co-editor, and that was that.

XIX

IT may seem that I am stressing to an unnecessary degree
slights, or imagined slights, from a man who on various
occasions had shown me kindness, and whom I exacerbated
by my lack of tact. But in all our later contacts Yeats
made it plain to me that I had incurred his displeasure,
nor was this in any way fanciful on my part. When he was
writing his life of Yeats, Hone remarked to me one day:
"You know you are always saying that Yeats disliked you,
so I think I can tell you this. I was going to include it in
my book, but then decided not to. Yeats said to someone,
'There are three people in Dublin whom I dislike. Dunsany
because he is rude to his wife in front of the servants,
Monk Gibbon because he is argumentative, and Sarah
Purser because she is a petulant old woman.' "

It was a true bill in my own case. I was argumentative,
although I did not often argue. Nevertheless my opposition
to his ideas, or my anxiety to get him to clarify them,
nearly always slipped out sooner or later. Even if I remained silent I believe that it could be felt. But it is typical
of W. B. that in his other two repugnances the reason was
entirely fictitious. Dunsany's behaviour in the domestic
circle could hardly have mattered as much as that to the
chivalrous ex-Senator. Dunsany's real crime was Lolly's
crime ("one of my sisters is a demon") and Sarah Purser's
crime, and everyone's crime who opposed the poet, even
over some trifle. I remember sitting with Sarah Purser in
her garden at Mespil House when she was ninety-one ("Do
you see that window up there? That is the window of the

room I intend to occupy when I am bedridden. It has a lovely view") and hearing from her own lips the whole story of her quarrel with Yeats. But, as so often happens with other people's quarrels and not our own, I did not give the matter my strict attention. It had all happened half a lifetime before, but Sarah—who even in her ninety-sixth year remained a person whom one could not have bested with impunity—had doubtless shown fight on the occasion, and so become one of W. B.'s three Dublin hates.

It was ironical that I should be another; I whose youth had been spent worshipping him from afar. Awe of him in the first instance—as Lily suggested—and, later, a certain sour refusal to play the part of a humbug even to a great man, by concealing or qualifying my views, or by disguising even a fraction of my devoted allegiance to A. E., had no doubt accounted for my gradual estrangement, and now I seemed to fall further and further from grace. My first prose book, *The Seals*, had come out and had been recommended by the Book Society. Unknown to me, Jonathan Cape had sent a set of page-proofs to A. E., whose approval was so generous that the publisher asked and got permission to print his letter on the back of the wrapper.

I sent a copy of *The Seals* to W. B., but it was not acknowledged by him, as its two predecessors had been. The letter on the cover stamped me unequivocally as one of A. E.'s canaries, and in the book itself there had been a trill or two in praise of that great man.

Lolly made one more effort to put matters right. The two sisters were growing old but they retained all their vitality and goodness of heart. Higgins used to annoy me by his stock, facetious allusion to them as "The Weird Sisters." They were not the weird sisters: anything less like the witches in *Macbeth* could scarcely be imagined than Lolly, still straight as a ramrod, energetic and voluble, or Lily with all her serene, immobile dignity. Lily was beginning to have very poor health. She suffered from some

171

bronchial trouble which made every breath she drew painful and noisy. Nevertheless she remained the most delightful and entertaining of hostesses, despite the loud, continuous sibilant reminder of distress. Whenever I came back to Dundrum I would pay her several visits. She would sit sunk deep in her huge armchair, the wireless within reach and a number of little tables near her. She still did some embroidery and she delighted in cutting the vividly coloured illustrations and advertisements out of American and other periodicals and pasting them into huge volumes bound up from sheets of stiff brown paper. One of these immense scrapbooks, with board covers of patterned paper, was given to my firstborn when he was two years old.

As they grew older and Lolly's nervous mannerisms, as well as Lily's bronchial disabilities, increased, it became harder for these two gallant women to live at such close quarters as the little two-storey house, Ghurteen Dhas, necessitated. One year I returned and Lily told me that they had worked out a plan by which they each lived independently, had their meals at different times and avoided overlapping in any way. Lily was more or less confined to a single room. Lolly, still busy with her printing, came and went. But each by mutual agreement lived a completely separate life. Their one surviving maid—now growing distinctly elderly herself—ministered to them both, but at different times and in different rooms. She adored Lily, but if Lolly's name was mentioned by me she would cast her eyes up to heaven and imply that it needed a saint out of heaven to survive the caprices of that volatile personality.

I can only say that both sisters remained as vital and charming as ever, where I was concerned. No doubt Lolly was fatiguing to live with, her relentless energy still bent on keeping the Cuala flag flying. And Lily's breathing had become so stressed that it would have been very difficult for any nervous or impatient person to endure it continually. And so they had worked out this solution, quietly, calmly

172

and with dignity. I enjoyed my visits to Lily as much as ever, prowling round the walls to study once more her various treasures, or listening to her as she described to me in the most natural and homely way certain visionary experiences which she had had at various times of her life.

For Lily was a visionary, and, years later, when discussing A. E.'s visions in a thesis for my doctorate I was glad to have had the benefit of my conversations with her, for they threw considerable light on the visionary process. There I quote her as saying: "I very seldom talk of these things, because people think that you are strange if you do." But in fact she accepted her experiences in very much the same way that we all accept our dreams. In dreams we have sensory experience—visual certainly, auditory after a fashion—without any use of the appropriate intermediary sense. We apprehend form without materiality; colour without light.

> Is it that minds, deep in their being, keep
> A fire of their own to use in sleep?

Utterly mystifying as this faculty is, and absurd as it renders any attempt to link consciousness to a series of purely materialistic stimuli, not one of us gets excited about it, or even pauses to consider how amazing it is, or what philosophic inferences might be drawn from it. In the same way Lily accepted her clairvoyance, said little about it, because it was liable to distress people, but regarded it as one more indication that there are more things in heaven and earth than are dreamt of in most men's philosophies. She was not anxious to theorise about it or to use it as propaganda for any particular view of the universe.

When I asked Lily were her visions as vivid and real as a particularly vivid dream, she replied that they were more so, because there was no "confusion" and complete continuity of event. In them she might actually feel the warmth of the sunlight and the transition in temperature

173

from sun to shadow. At the same time another part of consciousness would remain aware of her companions and surroundings in real life, so that she could have deliberately pulled herself back to them if she had wished.

Lily spoke to me of her visions, but she also lent me a typed account of them, of which I made use in my thesis. There I describe a series of four of her visions, separated from one another by an interval of several years, and quote her as saying:

In the late summer of 1895—I think—I was sitting in the dining-room of Blenheim Road, Bedford Park, London, with my father and three friends of his (Professor York Powell, Mr Nash and John O'Leary). They were all smoking and talking politics. I gave up listening to them and sat and looked at a matchbox which was on the table; it had a blue oblong end which was towards me. I thought that this opened and that I saw a flight of steps of very old worn stone; I thought that they led up from the sea and they were between two walls of houses, and it was bright sunlight . . . I walked up these steps and I could see into the houses, the windows were open, I thought they were full of people and life and movement, but all invisible to me. I turned to the left along a narrow street all paved with worn stones, and on my right there was a little old church. I went up the steps into the church. I felt distinctly the coldness and darkness after coming out of the bright sunshine, and then the figure of a man—whom I called in my own mind "The Messenger"—stepped forward as if he had been waiting.

He was dressed entirely in yellow draperies, like an Eastern dress. He walked up the middle of the church and I followed, and he took from the altar a white box covered all over with silver tracery; he opened the box and gave me out of it a red rose—a real rose but perfectly flawless. I took it and out of it came two tiny blue moths, they fluttered down the church and I and the Messenger followed.

I went out on the steps again and could feel the heat of the sun and the dazzling light after the gloom. The Messenger stepped back into the church, I stood on the steps holding the rose, the two moths flew back into the rose—the rose closing all its petals over them. Then all vanished.

174

All this time, Lily explained to me, she never lost touch completely with her environment; she was aware, that is to say, with one part of her mind of her father and his friends, and of the room she was sitting in, and she presumably possessed the power at any moment to break off the vision and rejoin them.

This was the first of a series of four visions all concerned with a different coloured rose, The Red Rose, The White Rose, The Yellow Rose and then a fourth vision—The Black Rose. The first took place about 1895, the second in January 1911, the third in the winter of 1922, and the fourth in 1924. A fifth vision on 5 July 1937 concerned the restoration of all four roses to a casket. In each of these visions a messenger in yellow robes met her—the location always different, twice a church, once a cathedral, once a temple in India, once another temple reached by a long flight of steps which she recognised years later from a picture of the Temple of the Thousand Steps in China. A. E. also had consecutive visions. In *The Candle of Vision* he speaks of "a second vision in the same series," "about five or six years after," as though with him too a vision could belong to a series separated by considerable intervals of time.

Only the visionary knows with any degree of accuracy what exactly happens to him, and even he may become doubtful of this experience after being for a time dependent upon his memory of it. But this description by Lily Yeats of a dual functioning of consciousness is borne out by a passage in Dom Butler's *Western Mysticism:* "St Gregory says that at the height of the vision St Benedict thrice called out with a loud voice to the Deacon Servandus, who was in the room beneath, to come up and see the wonder, and related to him what had occurred."

On one occasion when I and my wife were having tea with Lily she told us of another experience she had had. She had suddenly seen—it was at night and she was in bed,

175

propped up on pillows—a road with a woman's body lying amid bloodstains on one side of it. Then a little dog crept out from beneath the hedge at the side of the road, seized a hand which had been severed from the body and ran away with it in his mouth. It seemed an absurd and macabre incident to be the subject of a vision. But, as she learnt later, on that very night a young nun had been knocked down in the darkness by the Blessington steam-tram and killed. Her body was found but the hand was missing, a fact which caused considerable mystification to the coroner and his jury. Lily's comment to us was: "I could have told them what had happened."

Lily accepted her clairvoyance, or whatever the faculty was, as quietly and unconcernedly as she accepted the rest of life. She was as disinterested as ever, calm, generous, uncomplaining despite her distressing illness. I seem to remember her telling me that as a girl she had gone for a time to help with the children of a family in France. At any rate I know that now, late in life, she had taken to reading French books and was pleased to find that she had not forgotten the language. From time to time she wrote to me in Swanage. She had greeted the appearance of *The Seals* within a few days of its publication.

11 January 1935   Churchtown,
                                                                  Dundrum
                                                                  Co. Dublin

My dear Willy Monk

I have just read your book *The Seals* with great pleasure. Your descriptions of that first day of dazzling beauty, then the beauty a little dulled by the shooting of the birds, the slaughter of the seals (dulled but not destroyed because you feel excited by the chase) leading on to the dropping down and blotting out of rich colour, the warmth of the sun, the beauty of the whole scene, by the descent of the great grey clouds and the drizzling rain—all this is beautiful, but I think your digressions towards the end of the book spoil it a little, break into the flow and cause the reader's thoughts to stray away—look aside—and so miss the road as it were, the path from the beauty of the first day to the greyness and regrets of the end—which is what I think you must have meant your readers to feel.

It brought back to me the lovely honey-scented days when I was young and wandered for hours over the green lands by the Atlantic near Sligo. There is magic and colour and beauty—patches of wild thyme, lucky berry—tiny pansies like jewels—bright coloured snailshells.

When you are as old as I am you will have forgotten the grey days of rain and feel as I do that the sun always shone and that the everchanging colour was always deep and rich and lovely.

I am so glad to see the blue band on your book (Book Society Recommendation). This I hope will mean a second edition in no time.

Looking through a family album of small "visiting-card" mid-Victorian photographs at Ghurteen Dhas one afternoon I had come across one of a particularly beautiful young woman, wearing a crinoline. She was tall, fair and had a classically lovely face and yet an expression of great sweetness. "Who is this marvellous creature?" It appeared that she was their Aunt Grace. "And who did she marry?" It appeared that she had never married anyone. "What! this marvellous creature unmarried! 'Madame 'twere a sin, to die and leave the world no copy.' "

Lily added a postscript to her letter now:

P.S. My Aunt Grace, born in 1845, is slowly leaving us—no great suffering and we hope there will be none.

She was a beautiful woman when young and always a pleasure to see—had character and wit—she was bridesmaid to your grandmother—she told me that your grandmother wore a white bonnet trimmed with real orange-blossom, and as she wished to take it on her honeymoon with her, Aunt Gracie took out the real blossom and sewed in artificial roses and did it all in the drawing-room surrounded by the guests.

Lily kept a book of family dates and annals, destined to be of very considerable use to Yeats's biographers. My father had been interested in family history and had collected a certain amount of material, and I and Lily were able to exchange our gleanings. A large number of Lily's letters to me are on genealogical matters:

My dear Willy Monk

I am reading through the letters and making notes of who the "Yeats" writers were.

Except when they are writing about Tommy Taylor they are the most impersonal letters I ever read, were there other letters? in which they gave even a glimpse of their hearts, feeling, thoughts—and were these letters burnt? what do you think?

George says "you Yeats are far too impersonal." I don't know quite what she means.

This letter was written in May 1936. My father had died the previous year, and Lily continues:

I had a beautiful dream about your father the other night.

I saw a hillside—in it a well of deep crystal-clear water, full of light as if lit from beneath. I knew it was a symbol and meant "the living water" of the parable of the well in Samaria.

Then your father came and dipped a glass deep in the well and drank the water—drinking it with ecstasy—twice he drank of it —that was all—but it was beautiful and he happy, exalted. . . .

W. B. is better.* Michael came back to St C[olumba's] last Friday. Anne will wait and come back with her parents.

All good wishes and all good things to you and yours

Your affect cousin
Lily Yeats.

* This may have been the occasion when, as Lily told me, he had been put onto an exclusive diet of peaches and milk and was beginning to find it not only acceptable but perfectly sustaining.

XX

EIGHT months before this letter was written I had paid the least successful of all my various visits to W. B. Lolly had arranged it, kind-hearted as ever, and still hopeful that she would get me accepted in the fold. She probably had the forthcoming anthology in mind. At any rate it was settled between her and Mrs Yeats that I and my wife should go out to tea at Riversdale on Sunday afternoon, before I returned to my work in Dorset in mid-September. As we walked out along the road from Rath-farnham I said to my wife: "I always annoy Yeats by talking too much. Now this time I am going to be silent and let you do most of the talking."

It was a good resolution and for once I kept it. But, when we left two hours later, I was under no illusion as to its success. I was outside the pale, too far outside for even silence to avail me now. We had tea in front of the fire in the further of the two rooms. My wife told them something of our recent holiday in Donegal. Presently Gogarty arrived in company with an American lady who was on a visit to Ireland. He had just presented her with a copy of his *Collected Poems*, a gift she assured us she valued highly. Gogarty chattered away. I, with a seal upon my lips, scarcely ventured into the fray at all, and the American lady amused us with her impressions of Ireland. Presently Yeats got up from his chair and said slowly and with an almost rehearsed deliberation "Oh, Gogarty, I'm doing this *Cambridge [sic] Book of Modern Verse* and I don't want to overlook anything of yours. Have I got all your books?"

179

As he said it he gave—according to my wife who is the last person in the world to read malice into anyone else's action —a look, almost a leer in my direction, as though it were his deliberate intention to wound me. Gogarty responded with alacrity. He leaped out of his chair, dashed into the hall and retrieved the volume which he had just given his American friend. She would have to wait. No doubt it would be replaced in time. If the whole incident had been rehearsed with the special intent of pleasing one poet and humiliating another it could not have been carried out more effectively. We had been reminded that the anthology was in the course of making, that Yeats was going carefully and conscientiously over the whole field, and would omit nothing that could be thought of any value. As we said goodbye I could only put in a hurried word to Mrs W. B. in the passageway, reminding her that her husband had my books, and hoping that he would have a look at them. Higgins had already said a word in their favour, but if his advocacy had failed with the Broadsides, it was not very likely that he would succeed here.

He did not, and I had little hope that he would. Even my successful resolution to avoid all argument had been mis-interpreted, for when Lolly rang me up a few days later, she informed me: "They liked your wife but they said that you talked nothing but commonplaces." In a subsequent letter she seems to have forgotten this, for I find her writing to me optimistically:

I hope your visit to Rathfarnham was a success. What about the Anthology? You, like Oliver Gogarty, should have gone armed with your poems. Will you see W. B. again? I am very glad to hear from Lily what a beautiful window is to be the form the memorial to your father is to take. Instead of missing the Canon less, as time goes on—I believe we of the parish miss him more—he *kept up* all our hearts—his courage was inspiring —*everyone* felt it—spiritual courage of a very high order.

Your affectionate cousin
Lolly Yeats.

Exclusion from the series of broadsides was a trifle. Exclusion from the Academy was a disappointment, and I remember how my father argued that it would be more creditable to be elected freely at some later date than to have been nominated in the first instance. But exclusion from the anthology was a definite blow.

In the very first sentence of his introduction to the book Yeats was to write, "I have tried to include in this book all good poets who have lived or died from three years before the death of Tennyson to the present moment, except two or three who belong through the character of their work to an earlier period." That is definitive enough for anyone, although he qualified it later. If one's name was not there, it was because one's work was negligible. Yeats had praised one of my poems in the *Irish Statesman*, he had spoken well of my work both to me and to his sisters at various times, he had presumably sanctioned my Tailteann Silver Medal, and he had allowed Lennox Robinson to include two of my poems in his small Cuala anthology which had been published as a postscript to *A Golden Treasury of Irish Verse* for those whose work had come into notice subsequently. Of the seven pages and nine poems devoted, say, to Ernest Dowson in *The Oxford Book of Modern Verse* it should have been possible—had I been worthy—to omit one, and to include eight or twelve lines of mine. Or, if that was not possible, he might perhaps have spared a quatrain from the three pages and seven poems allotted to Margot Ruddock, or one of the seventeen poems by Gogarty that he prints, fine poet as the latter is.

But it is curious—all the Irish poets with whom Yeats had quarrelled or who stood in his disfavour were omitted from the book. I do not think he had ever quarrelled with Katharine Tynan, but she had fallen from grace, and, though her work is to be found in the original *Oxford Book of Verse*, it is omitted in the anthology compiled by the friend of her youth, which covers, not eight or nine

181

centuries of poetic activity, but merely the years of her life-time. Dunsany is omitted. Austin Clarke, another Tailteann medallist, who has done as much for poetry in Ireland as any man now living, but who had opposed Yeats on various occasions in the Academy, is not there. And, most striking omission of all, Seumas O'Sullivan is not there. His case is worth discussing. An authentic poet whose work has always kept to traditional paths, his work has been in multitudinous anthologies on both sides of the Atlantic, and I remember his telling me that a single poem of his had brought him in £50 in anthology fees in a single year. Yeats by making him one of the seven foundation members of his Academy had recognised his importance. The fact that they had since quarrelled made it not less but more necessary that he should not appear to be penalising a man whom he disliked. *Noblesse oblige*, if nothing else, should have suggested that, however modest the representation, his name should be there.

Mrs Yeats, loyal as ever to her husband's memory, told me some years ago of a letter she had come across from Sturge Moore which proved that W. B. had consulted him as to O'Sullivan's inclusion or exclusion, and that Sturge Moore—hardly an authority on Irish poets—gave his verdict against him. But it does not make it very much better for Yeats to have made Sturge Moore his conscience in the matter. And the English poet was probably not uninfluenced by what he thought Yeats wished.*

* In his preface to the book Yeats regrets the absence from it of Robert Graves, through circumstances "beyond my control." Graves himself gave the circumstances in his sixth Clark Lecture at Cambridge, which he prints in *The Crowning Privilege* (p. 117):
 While in Majorca, he wrote asking Laura Riding and myself, as co-authors of *A Survey of Modernist Poetry*, for advice: which younger English poets should he include in his new anthology? We suggested James Reeves, whose first book we had just published. Yeats rejected Reeves with this really devilish comment: "Too reasonable, too truthful. We poets should be good liars, remembering always that the Muses are women and prefer the embraces of gay, warty lads." So we declined to contribute ourselves.

Desmond MacCarthy described the anthology as "this book of strange omissions and strange inclusions." Hone in his biography writes, "It shows partiality to friends of the moment and to old friends. Some of these friends Yeats admires, and rightly so, but he does Lady Gregory, for instance, a doubtful service by inserting several pages of her translations from Hyde's Irish while rejecting certain others (in some cases members of his own Irish Academy!) who in courtesy merited at least a poem."

I will not discuss my own claims, if any. Higgins made one last effort on my behalf, asking Yeats to include "The Babe" which—quoted in *The Seals*—a number of people had thought highly of. But the reply was: "No, it is too late. It is all settled now."

I may seem to be making a big mountain out of a relatively small literary molehill. I may even seem to be evincing all the acute symptoms of author's persecution mania. But the uninitiated should realise that the prestige value of Yeats's anthology, at the time when it appeared, was enormous. If you were not there, you were no-one; if you were there, you had received the imprimatur of the greatest living poet. For years afterwards the effect of the book was felt. Makers of anthologies tend to favour familiar pastures. The herb there tastes sweetest to them. Every poet wants to be read, and on this particular occasion readers were going to be legion. The book came out, was widely reviewed, and soon W. B. could tell Lily that it had already sold sixty thousand copies. Those of us who were not between its covers could dwell on the melancholy reflection that we had lost not sixty thousand but three or four or five or six times that number of readers by our exclusion.

Like Edward Martyn, who never investigated *Hail and Farewell*, saying "George Moore is a very pleasant fellow but if I read his book I could no longer meet him," Austin Clarke took the very private revenge of never opening the anthology. I myself read it and noted in my journal, some time later:

Like all "personal" anthologies it is interesting as a reflection of its selector's mind, probably more interesting than a more conscientious or expected selection without personal bias. As such I enjoy it. The inclusion of Synge's translations and Frank O'Connor's wonderful "What shall we do for timber?" (from the Irish) delights me. The very fact that I enjoy much of it adds a little drop of gall to my disappointment that my name is not there, and I derive only a slight degree of comfort from Quiller-Couch's snort of rage at the mere mention of the book, or from Desmond MacCarthy's description of it.

Coming back to the book now after a twenty-year interval I give much the same verdict. It is always more difficult to arrange a chronological anthology than one where poems of similar mood or theme can be grouped together, as in Robinson's *Golden Treasury of Irish Verse* or Richard Church's admirable volume in Everyman's Library. Church and his fellow-anthologist link their poems in the most skilful way. They throw the net wide, but reveal continual sensitivity to similarities of mood and feeling in different poems; whereas Yeats tends to reveal caprice and a predilection for what had pleased him in the 1890's. Hal Summers's "Eclogue" written in our time and printed by Church is a greater poem, I feel, than anything that Yeats has from Dowson or Henley or Michael Field or Lionel Johnson. In his preface Yeats, who had included nothing of his own written before the age of forty, pontificated, speaking a little as though the fumes from the Delphic cave were in his nostrils. A lot of his generalisations are highly questionable:

We [the Irish Poets] have more affinity with Henley and Blunt than with other modern English poets, but have not felt their influence; we are what we are because almost without exception we have had some part in public life in a country where public life is simple and exciting ... I have a distaste for certain poems written in the midst of the great war ... passive suffering is not a theme for poetry . . . I have said nothing of my own work, not from modesty, but because writing through fifty years I have been now of the same school with John Synge and James Stephens, now in that of Sturge Moore and the younger "Michael Field:" and though the concentration of philosophy and social passion of the school of Day Lewis and in MacNeice lay beyond my desire, I would, but for a failure of talent, have been in that of Turner and Dorothy Wellesley.

Nonsense, all nonsense. For nearly fifty years he had been far too fine a poet to be in any school save his own.

XXI

A. E. had died in July 1935, a few months after
my father. I had seen him in London earlier in the year
and I was staying with my wife's parents at Bonchurch in
the Isle of Wight, only a couple of hours by paddle-steamer
from Bournemouth, when he died there. Next day the
Irish Times devoted almost the whole of its main news
page to him, including an admirable tribute from Gogarty
who had visited him before his death. No Irish writer—not
even Yeats himself—has received, in my time, so many
columns from the press. His body was taken back to
Ireland for burial beside his wife at Mount Jerome. De
Valera and many famous Irishmen were present. Yeats
stood at the graveside but he refused to make any funeral
oration. He was reported to have declared: "If I spoke at
all I would have to speak the bad as well as the good."
Frank O'Connor spoke in his place. Yeats's whole behaviour at the time was strange. There had been some
talk of spreading the Irish tricolour on the coffin. Yeats
declared if this was done he would snatch it away with his
own hands. It was from Mrs Curran that I learnt this, but
there is some reference to it, I think, in one of his letters to
Dorothy Wellesley. Did he think it would give the funeral
a political significance, or had he some innate objection to
flags, for, describing his daughter Anne's association with
the Girl Guides, he said to me, "I let her go in for all of
it. Except of course the Union Jack part. I won't have
that."

At a meeting of the Academy some weeks later Yeats,

according to Austin Clarke, made a few cursory references to his dead friend, "A great journalist! A great journalist!" and then launched forth on a twenty-minute eulogy of T. E. Lawrence who had recently been killed on his motor-bicycle.

The relation between Yeats and A. E. was a curious one, and in one sense a mystery. If it is possible for one man to be jealous of another without knowing it, Yeats was jealous of A. E. Lennox Robinson has said to me: "I used to see the two of them hobnobbing happily together by the fire like two old cronies. Then some stranger might come in and instantly Yeats would set out to make A. E. look small." Yeats grudged A. E. his many disciples. I think that this was so, long before Moore wrote *Hail and Farewell* and drew the pleasing portrait there of the maieutic A. E. According to Hone, Yeats

thought of Balzac's phrase, "barren rascals," applied to critics, when he considered A. E.'s Sunday evenings in Rathgar or George Moore's Saturdays. He pronounced a hasty judgement, afterwards withdrawn, upon James Stephens, now rising to fame. "Colum," he noted in his journal, "is the one victim of George Russell's misunderstanding of life that I rage over."

To be A. E.'s man was about the worst recommendation anyone could have with Yeats. They had been friends as boys, had influenced each other enormously as young men, and to the end of his life the Willie Yeats, whose image A. E. cherished, was almost certainly the youth with the virgin beard with whom he had once discussed all things in heaven and earth. But their ways had parted at quite an early stage. A. E. had no interest in spiritualism, very little indeed in occultism as such, and I have already quoted the letter to Yeats in which he says that the latter's "mysticism" is certainly not his. There ensued a nine-year gap in their correspondence after Yeats had tried to bully A. E. into withdrawing his pledged word to Dudley Digges.

187

In their sixties, both with well-established reputations, they made a wonderful conversational couple. It was like watching the encounter of two demiurges of totally different temperament. To some extent they played up to one another on these occasions.

A. E. had an enormous admiration for Yeats's poetry. Again and again he wrote of it in the *Irish Statesman* with perception and enthusiasm. Yeats thought highly of his friend's poems, and in his anthology made a discerning selection. What rankled I believe with Yeats was that A. E. stood for something that had once existed in W. B. also, but which he had sacrificed in the course of his career. Yeats had followed the path of art. A. E. had followed the path of personal attainment. When he died, Mrs W. B. very pertinently remarked to her husband: "A. E. was the nearest to a saint that you and I are ever likely to know. You are a better poet, but you are not a saint."

Once again that generous and perceptive individual showed her good sense. W. B. probably approved her words, for he quotes them in a letter to Dorothy Wellesley. But subconsciously they may have rankled. Pamela Travers, who nursed A. E. with such devotion at Bournemouth during the last few weeks of his life, tells me that he wrote to his boyhood friend soon after getting there. The days went by. Still there was no answer from Willie Yeats. Each day A. E. would make the same enquiry, until finally Pamela Travers despatched a telegram begging the poet to write. Only then at the very end did the longed-for letter arrive.

It was not only Plato's ghost who stood at the successful poet's elbow muttering "What then?" It was A. E. himself who did so. One might almost say that A. E. *was* Plato's ghost. Yeats had dabbled in religious speculation. A. E. had practised the religious virtues, so that Roman Catholics and men of all creeds had gathered at the graveside of this theosophically-minded heretic. Yeats had spun a magic web out of the perfect metrical phrase. A. E. had voiced

> Truths too deep
> For men's denying

in prose, lucid, simple and irradiated with inner spiritual significance. Yeats, with the insatiable desire of some temperaments to fill all parts, would have liked to be A. E. as well as himself. But Fortune, even in her most prodigal mood, cannot pour wholly opposite gifts from her horn of plenty. He had chosen, and A. E. had chosen, and each had fully vindicated his particular choice. Yeats's attitude to A. E. in later life was a mixture of friendship and irritation. They had had fierce quarrels at different times; Yeats abhorred opposition from any quarter, and it is possible too that Moore's flattering treatment of A. E. in *Hail and Farewell*, which contrasted with that of Yeats, as well as the affection and veneration which A. E. inspired in the younger generation, may have seemed excessive to him. When in 1932 Yeats came to review *Song and its Fountains* in the *Spectator* he revealed some of his sense of irritation:

One opens a friend's book with dread, every trick of style has its associations, we wonder perpetually—such hatred is in friendship—how a man we have buckled to our heart can have so little sense. Admiration can but feed hatred, and if we have known the man for five-and-forty years and met him once a week for the last ten, and must write about his book—and what else can be so interesting?—it may seem best to touch upon some one aspect and ignore the rest. Yet, in writing about A. E.'s *Song and its Fountains* I cannot do so; I must face all my associations, merely stating at the outset that my hatred has won the right to call itself friendship.

Most friends would dissent from this. Whatever may be the psychological affiliations of love and hatred, the latter does not seem the customary component of friendship. Yeats's review of the book is a carping affair with a paragraph of recantation at the end. It has none of the penetration

189

shown in A. E.'s many reviews of Yeats's work in the columns of the *Irish Statesman*. Indeed at times it seems a confession of latent antipathy. When he wrote *The Trembling of the Veil* Yeats was younger and less conscious of this hostility, and the portrait which he drew there is worth studying because it contains lights as well as shadows. It contains much generous praise, but there are reservations. Even there he writes:

We are never satisfied with the maturity of those whom we have admired in boyhood and, because we have seen the whole circle—even the most successful life is but a segment—we remain to the end their harshest critic . . . I demanded of Russell some impossible things.

It is possible that it was the apotheosis of A. E. in the evening of his life that annoyed Yeats most of all; but they had had their differences of opinion always, for though A. E. loved Yeats (and he did), when he came up against a certain dictatorial, tyrannical streak in the poet he rebelled and showed an obstinacy quite equal to the occasion.

The conscious or unconscious rivalry with A. E. is strikingly revealed in a story told by L. A. G. Strong in *Scattering Branches*. After telling us that Yeats's last play *The Herne's Egg* is a riot of copulation and other men's jokes, lit by flashes of tremendous and erratic poetry, Strong goes on:

Several critics have attributed this to the gland operation which he underwent some five or six years before he died. One can imagine his smile at such a superficiality. The life of a man of genius is not so easily charted. The operation did not change his life's current. Instead we must look to that in him which made him demand the operation: to the manner of man he was.

He said to me once, after he had undergone it, "A. E. should have the operation," and added swiftly, "He would never consent to it, he would die sooner."

Quite so. It is a case of Plato's ghost once more. Always this comparison with the standards or the outlook of this

190

friend of his youth. Why should he make such a proposal at such a moment unless a subconscious sense of rivalry brought the name to his lips. And how sound his diagnosis. A. E. would have died first, simply because he would have thought it below the dignity of the seer to worry too much about the affairs of the body, most of all where they concerned carnal activity. He held with Plotinus that we had descended into matter, that it was right for a man to love, right for him to marry and engender children. But, not even for the sake of increased artistic productivity, still less for the mere pleasures of this poor flesh, should a man of sixty-four take advantage of surgical ingenuity to renew in some measure his virility.

I do not pass judgment on Yeats. No-one knows the particular psychological problems of another, especially where sex is concerned. I have a lurking admiration for his wild old wicked man who knows that God can draw men to him through the flame of suffering, but who declares defiantly:

> But a coarse old man am I,
> I choose the second best.

I am even ready to admit, so strange are the interwoven ramifications of the various forms of energy, sexual, intellectual and aesthetic, even religious, that an increase of one frequently has, or may have, its influence upon the others. But for the philosopher there are no short cuts. A. E. was a seer first and an artist second; and Yeats was right when he said that he would never have sought sexual recrudescence, even if it held out promise of a renewal of inspiration. Inspiration for him had no link with Priapus. It was part of the supreme mystery. It was part of "the flight of the Alone to the Alone."

XXII

I COME now to the last of my contacts with Yeats and will try to relate it, if not dispassionately, at least with fairness. A. E. had died in July. In the last letter he wrote to his son Diarmuid he had suggested that, if his life were written, Padraic Colum would be a suitable biographer, and that if his work for the *Irish Statesman* were to be edited and republished it should be done by me. A few years before I had suggested to him that much treasure trove was available there, and that it should be possible to create a book of varied opinions, somewhat on the plan of Eckermann's *Conversations with Goethe*. I made a preliminary survey and produced some pages of sample extracts. The plan was mentioned to Yeats, who deprecated it, and A. E. decided not to go on with it. He would wait, and perhaps do something with the various essays and reviews himself. He sent me a cheque for my labours which I returned, but was rewarded with a picture instead.

After his death Diarmuid Russell wrote to me, asking me if I would undertake the book. I replied that I would, provided that I might do a full-scale profile of A. E. as introduction. The book I had in mind would range over his many fields of thought. To appreciate it fully a reader would need to have a picture of him in mind. Colum was asked to do the biography, but refused, owing to the pressure of other work, and John Eglinton was presently asked to undertake it. I explained to Diarmuid Russell that I had once essayed a selection, but on a rather different plan, that the few pages done then might still be in existence, among

GEORGE RUSSELL (A. E.)

his father's papers, and that, if he could find them, they might be a help to me; but that the new book would be on wholly different lines, that many of the selections would be much longer, some of them might be complete, and that the attempt to weave them into a series of conversations or discussions would be abandoned. Russell agreed with all this, and I wrote accordingly to Messrs Macmillan.

I was in Dublin again for a time after my father's death. My mother had moved to a house in Palmerston Road and I was staying with her there. One morning the post brought me a letter from Diarmuid Russell in America, saying that he had found the half-dozen pages or so of manuscript and would like to show them to W. B. Curran and someone else —I think Pamela Travers. I thought no more of the matter. I know Con Curran, one of A. E.'s closest and most loyal friends, but W. B. Curran meant nothing to me at all. He was welcome to see the manuscript, whoever he might be, not that it was of any great significance by now.

Thanks to this neglect of punctuation on my part, or on Diarmuid Russell's, the bombshell when it did arrive exploded with all the more shattering violence. A few weeks later I opened another letter from Diarmuid at the breakfast table and learnt from it that W. B. had read my manuscript notes, that he did not approve of them, and that he would like Pamela Travers to edit a short selection from the same material for the Cuala Press, which he did not think could interfere at all with mine. Diarmuid Russell—very honourably—had said that he could not do such a thing without my consent and Macmillan's. He now wrote to ask me for it. He admitted that he would very much like to see the Cuala book and he had told W. B. that I would get in touch with him.

It was the last straw. I had been excluded from the broadsides. I had not been found worthy of the anthology. When I spoke I was argumentative, and when I put a curb on my tongue I spoke nothing but commonplaces. And now the one task entrusted to me by A. E. himself was to be taken from me and given to someone else, by that all-powerful old plotter, who disliked me and lost no opportunity of putting a spoke in my wheel. It was nonsense to say that a Cuala book would not interfere with mine. It would skim all the cream off the material, and my book, following hard upon it, would be a complete anticlimax, a mere gathering up of the leavings. It seemed to me that deliberate tyrannical interference could scarcely go further. It would have needed Nathan the prophet to express my feelings on this proposed theft of my one remaining ewe-lamb.

Yeats was a great poet and I had given him my lifelong homage. But this was too much. I had no redress. I was helpless. I rang up a couple of friends. I walked as far as Garville Avenue to consult the kindly Con Curran. All he could say was, what I knew already, that Yeats was such a formidable antagonist that almost anything one did was certain to be wrong. W. B. held all the cards. He always held them. I was to be quietly shouldered out of the way. I was to be jostled off the pathway into the gutter where I rightly belonged. Poking his head forward and gazing at me through the gold rims of his glasses, Curran volunteered: "Some people say that Yeats is really timid, that if you lose your temper with him he caves in. I don't know . . ."

No, the one thing I must not do was lose my temper. I had the poet's own word for it that the excitable man is never the strong man. The fact that I longed to shout insults at him and to throw a brick through his window was the very strongest argument for not going anywhere near him. But what was I to do? There was nothing to do. He held all the cards and he was playing them with his usual skill.

In the end I sat down and wrote to Macmillan's. I told them of Yeats's suggestion. I told them that he had seen my brief original sample manuscript and that he did not like it, but I added that it must not be taken as representative of the treatment of the present book, where most of the pieces would be considerably longer. And having told them the facts I left the decision in their hands.

I had done the right thing. I had never hoped to outplay Yeats in his own suit, which was the deft achievement of his designs with the minimum of fuss and the maximum scornful overriding of an opponent's point of view. But for once I was to have the satisfaction of trumping his ace. I had felt myself helpless. I had felt—absurd as it may seem —that, just as he had refrained from speaking at A. E.'s graveside, so he was now going to come between A. E. and his posthumous fame by side-tracking into a small hand-printed edition what should reach a far larger audience, and by taking all the heart out of my enterprise before I ever began it.

Two mornings later—by return of post—I received a long envelope from Macmillan's. They were Yeats's own publishers, but that did not blind them, I imagine, to certain of his traits. They wrote that they would not under any circumstances approve a Cuala book and they enclosed an agreement for my book which they had signed and which they now asked me to sign.

I was saved. I took my five-year-old son and three-year-old daughter up the road as far as the leafy pleasaunces of Palmerston Park, one of those small but verdurous public parks dotted about the suburbs of Dublin and created for the benefit of a particular neighbourhood. As they played there on the grass or watched the other children on the swings and see-saws, it seemed to me that my own mood that morning was as carefree, as confident as that of any child in the gardens, such are the extremes of feelings that poets know, which carry them from the sulphurous darkness of yesterday to the serene matutinal calm of today. I no longer cared about Yeats's anthology. I no longer cared whether he thought my conversation commonplace or not; all I cared about now was to abandon my own literary work for the moment and make a really good book out of the material that A. E. had seen fit to entrust to me.

I had won my case. The matter was settled. Macmillan's said that they had had letters from Diarmuid Russell which made it quite clear that the book should be entrusted to me, if I chose to do it. I was not going to debate it further with anyone, least of all Yeats. I signed my agreement, posted it back to Harold Macmillan and, I rather imagine, said a prayer for his welfare in this world and the next.

But there was to be a curious sequel. My opponent was never one to fling down his cards and concede the remaining tricks. Lolly informed me presently that W. B. had gone off to London on his way to Majorca where he was to winter. But this must have been a mistake on her part, for going to the Abbey Theatre with my wife the following Saturday evening, we were surprised to see, from our seats in the front row of its single balcony, Mrs Yeats enter the stalls, followed a moment later by W. B. At the Abbey it was almost *de rigueur* for the occupants of the stalls to turn presently in their seats and take a good look round the house—stalls and balcony included—to see whether any familiar faces were present. I saw Mrs Yeats do this now, I saw her gaze radiate slowly along the high obstructive brass rail of the balcony until it reached us. A moment later I saw her lean over and say something to W. B.

I was like a soldier who, having been almost blasted from the face of the veld by his repeated and indiscreet quickness on the trigger, has now at last learnt the value of holding his fire. I said to my wife: "I don't want Yeats to think that I am avoiding him. When the interval comes I shall go down to the entrance foyer. If he is there and wishes to speak to me, well and good. But I shall not speak to him first."

When the interval came I did this. The great man was already there, standing in dignified contemplation in front of the small fireplace. I stood a few yards away, chatting to friends. Yeats was extremely short-sighted and may not have seen me. I rather think that he did. But in this I may be wrong. Presently he turned and began to contemplate the fire. The bell went and I returned to my seat. During the second interval I remained in my seat.

But next day, Sunday, Mrs Yeats rang us up about five o'clock. I was out but my wife answered the telephone. "Oh, we saw your husband in town the other day. W. B. would like to talk to him." "I'll tell him. He will ring you." I returned, was given the message and rang them half an hour later. Yes, I could come out to Riversdale any time, tonight after supper if that suited them. Yes, eight o'clock. That would be fine.

Polonius declared that once being in a quarrel one should pursue it vigorously, but my female relatives, including my wife, thought otherwise. Before leaving for Riversdale I was implored repeatedly to keep my self-control. "Don't get angry. Be dignified. Don't lose your temper."

I obeyed them to the letter, and for years after I regretted it. If I had got really angry, if I had stormed and shouted, if I had said: "You hate me and I know you hate me, but, damn it all, there are some things one does not do even to those one hates. Whenever you have injured me hitherto, you have been completely within your rights. You are under no obligation to publish me, you are under no obligation to show any approval of my work if you have ceased to approve it. But having pushed me into the poetic gutter you have no right to jump on my face. A. E. wished me to do this book. I was his choice for it. You meddling old bastard, couldn't you leave me even this one piece of work to do, which your friend had assigned to me?"

These are the kind of words with which angry men— earthbound still—try to rid themselves of their anger. One

197

can expel rage by sheer holiness if one is a saint. Or one can try and rid oneself of it by an outburst which may only make bad worse. But to bottle it up is dangerous. Blake knew it and said, better to murder a baby in its cradle than to nurse unacted desires. Anger remains and festers in the heart. If I had shouted or raged at Yeats I might have exorcised the demon. As it was I remained dignified and—God forgive me—still feel angry after twenty years.

And yet I had never had such a cordial welcome at Riversdale. I arrived to find Mrs Yeats—bless her heart, it is a wife's mission to support her husband in all his designs, and to pour oil on the troubled waters when it is needed—all smiles and W. B. more cordial than I had ever known him. Normally I should have responded instantly and warmheartedly to such treatment. Now it was wasted on me. I awaited events. I had learnt my lesson at last, the lesson of silence. If anyone came out of hiding it must be the enemy. I was not going to mention Diarmuid Russell, Macmillan's, the book, even A. E., unless they were first mentioned to me. Yeats must introduce the topic and not I.

And so we sat in front of the fire and chatted amicably about indifferent things, while I waited wonderingly for the subject to be broached which had brought me there. The time went by, and it was now that I heard about Anne's activities with the Girl Guides and the poet's views on flags. At last after about twenty minutes the poet took the plunge: "Diarmuid Russell has written to me . . . he would like, if you agree, for me to . . ." and so on.

It was the moment for me to produce my ace. I said quietly: "Oh yes. I've written to Macmillan's and told them of the position, but they say that they would prefer that there was not another book. They've sent me an agreement and I've signed it, and I a little resented your suggestion that the book should be taken out of my hands and given to Miss Travers."

He raised himself in his chair a little.

"What's that? What's that?"

"I a little resented"—slowly and as distinctly as any words could be spoken—"the suggestion that Pamela Travers should do the book."

He pooh-poohed this in a placatory fashion, saying that Pamela Travers was not a friend of theirs, and that he was perfectly willing for me to do it for Cuala.

It was at this point that I felt most disposed to disregard my family's admonitions and lose my temper. First I was to be jockeyed out of position without consideration. Then, when this proved impossible, Pamela Travers was to be quickly discarded; we were to come to terms; and only Macmillan's and A. E. himself (for I felt that any Cuala book would make the later book a damp squib) were to be the ultimate sufferers. It was barefaced. Yeats would not even have bothered to consult me on the matter had not Diarmuid Russell's loyalty to me and to his own father's expressed wish made this eventually necessary. I was in the position of a man knocked to the ground, and then, when his co-operation appears essential, picked up, dusted and given a friendly chuck under the chin. "I must smooth him down. I must smooth him down!"

My trump had been played quietly, not flung on the table. Macmillan's did not wish it; and that was all. Would Cuala not do another book about A. E., I suggested. Could they not, for example, translate Simone Téry's excellent essay on him?

"We never do translations," Mrs Yeats said.

"What about the Italian man whom Hone translated?"

"Oh, Rossi knew so much English he was almost English himself."

It would have been contrary to almost all precedent if I had been in Yeats's company for an hour without some dispute, open or implied, and the present occasion was no exception. A. E.'s famous open letter to Rudyard Kipling happened to be mentioned, and I said that it seemed to

199

me a stagy, melodramatic affair, altogether overworded.
Kipling's poem on Ulster is a piece of intolerance, gibing
savagely at most Irishmen. But A. E.'s letter (in which he
reproaches his fellow-poet for putting "Copyrighted in the
United States of America" at the end of his verses) is
fustian also, and rather absurd. Its whole tone of melodrama is indicated in its closing words:

You have smitten with all your might at creatures who are
frail on earth but mighty in the heavens, at generosity, at truth,
at justice, and heaven has withheld vision and power and beauty
from you, for this your verse is but a shallow newspaper article
made to rhyme. Truly ought the golden spurs to be hacked
from your heels and you to be thrust out of the Court.

The letter belonged to the year 1912 when passions ran
high, and Kipling's Norman self-righteousness, with its
usual charge that the Irish are smiling traitors who stab
you in the back (whereas the English mow you down in
a gentlemanly fashion with a machine-gun from in front),
afforded some excuse. Yeats immediately defended it. It
was a fine letter. Was I going to use it in my book? If not,
might he use it? I would not even concede this, saying
first that I would have to consider it, and then pointing out
that it had already been reprinted in A. E.'s *Imaginations
and Reveries*. We could agree about nothing. The talk
turned to A. E.'s poetry, but here again we were immediately at loggerheads. I thought that a good deal of the
earlier poetry was typical of the epoch and lacked lasting
quality. Yeats defended it. I preferred the later work and
I thought A. E.'s prose superb, the prose of *The Interpreters* and of the books that followed. For me it possessed
the inner radiance of a Donegal landscape, lit as it were
from within; lit, in this case, by spiritual light. Yeats surprised me by his eloquent advocacy of the poetry, but said
nothing about the merits of the prose, and that phrase "a
great journalist" still rankled in my mind, for I saw A. E.
as a mystic and a seer.

At last I rose to go. But Yeats was never one to relax his tenacious purpose, so long as it seemed to him that any hope was left. He made one more attempt to carry his point. Standing by his chair by the fireplace he remarked, "Well, we couldn't have given you very much on the book, but a royalty of $12\frac{1}{2}$ per cent on an edition of 400 is quite worth having." He had failed to push me out of his way; he had failed to win me; now there was just a chance that I might be hard up, and could be bought. In my resentment, and in all that acute sensitivity best described perhaps as persecution mania, it seemed to me that he was prepared to do anything, even to appeal to what he hoped might be my poverty, to get his way, print his little book, and, incidentally, ruin all prospects for the one which would follow it.

Once again it might have been better for me to get it all off my chest. But, apart from the admonitions I had received, one cannot lose one's temper where bitterness is the prevailing emotion. The more indignant one feels, the greater the restraint that seems to be laid on one's lips.

I did not lose my temper. I said coldly and quietly:

"Oh, I don't think we could have done that. Macmillan's are quite decided on the point. But in any case, having once offered the job to Miss Travers, I think you would have had to keep faith with her."

That was that. We said good night, and I was never to see Yeats again. Characteristically he made one more attempt to right the matter. Those who are sensitive themselves are often astonishingly but quite unconsciously insensitive to the feelings of others. I am well aware of this myself. All that had happened and has been related as seen through my eyes, and felt through my pulses, no doubt looked a good deal different to the eyes of Yeats. He did not like me, he had probably wounded me deliberately in the Gogarty incident; but it was not the business of a great poet to worry too much about the feelings of an argumentative

young man who lacked the manners to keep his mouth
shut when it would have been wiser to do so. Why should
he include me in his anthology when plenty of other poets,
as good or better, were being left out?

Only in this matter of the A. E. book had perhaps the
full measure of my resentment been brought home to him,
and the fact that he had acted ungenerously. "I must
smooth him down."

At any rate Lolly rang up next day. I must not mis-
understand W. B. He did not wish to be unkind to people
ever. And so on. Once again bitterness froze anger completely on my tongue. I accepted all these protestations
politely but without comment. It was too late for the olive
branch. W. B.'s gentler aspects did not interest me. I
thanked Lolly for ringing. It was obvious that she had been
in communication with Riversdale and was playing the part
of peacemaker, but, however well-intentioned it may have
been, this last fly cast across the nose of the trout that had
felt the barb, had no further attraction, and it was clear
from my manner that I did not wish to pursue the topic.

XXIII

ONLY to Lily did I voice my feelings fiercely on several occasions, telling her how bitterly I resented W. B.'s move to anticipate and so ruin the chances of my book. Her reply was always the same: "You must forget it. He is a great man and your cousin." To be the victim of greatness and consanguinity may perhaps take the sting out of a wrong for some people, but it didn't for me.

I did not forget. I did not forgive. But the revenge which I took upon the oppressor was a very modest one. It showed, I hope, that I was without pettiness. Into my book I gathered all the many wise and generous things that A. E. had said about Yeats in the *Irish Statesman*. They are all there, to a total of more than twenty pages. It was proof at least that I did not allow personal feeling into my literary transactions. And then, in my introduction, I allowed myself one moment of restrained malice, quoting the phrase from Simone Téry's essay: "*Ce qu'on aime le mieux dans Yeats, ce sont ces vers. Mais le chef-d'œuvre d'A. E., qui est un grand artiste, c'est encore lui-même.*" That was all, but it said everything. And the thrust was for W. B.'s own eye rather than for that of the general reader.

I gave up work on my own book *Mount Ida* and for nearly a year my wife and I laboured on the bound volumes of the *Irish Statesman* which Macmillan's had sent to me in Dorset. There was any amount of material. No rewriting was necessary but an enormous amount of rearrangement and cutting. As Harry Norman once said to me, "A. E. wrote for the *Statesman* with the speed of a man driving a motor-car. Daily, weekly, monthly, down it went on paper and was carried off to the printer with scarcely a word revised." He tended to repeat himself and many of his contributions were on the same or similar themes. Sometimes we amalgamated them. Even some of the longer articles we often recast. Some paragraphs were shed. Others were numbered in an order quite different from the original. Then the rearranged and numbered passages were typed in their new order. No word was ever added, except perhaps a conjunction; but we might begin with the last paragraph of an article and end with the first. This was not going to be journalism at all, but the distilled wisdom of A. E.'s maturity. Harold Macmillan loved A. E.; he had a crayon-illustrated letter from him framed on his mantelpiece; and his letters to me at this time are full of his interest and concern for the book. He had converted me from the format I had wished to one infinitely more suitable; and he agreed readily with me that Oliver Sheppard's head of A. E. in white marble—now in the National Gallery of Ireland—should be engraved by Emery Walker and used as a vignette for the title-page.

It was a fairly large book, beginning with my eighty-page portrait of A. E. of which L. A. G. Strong was to write, "He has prefaced it with a Memoir which will not be surpassed, for his mind is suited as few others to receive A. E.'s impress and respond to it." There followed three hundred pages of A. E. himself, divided into five main sections and a shorter section of so-called Aphorisms—gleanings, paragraphs or mere sentences from more ephemeral book-reviews. Even there one could find much wisdom:

"The poetic nature is like the weathercock on the spire, it catches the first breath of a changing wind. Tell me what the poets are saying today and we will know what the mass will be dreaming of in the next generation."

"The intuitions of a poetical nature are more exciting and profound than any logical philosophy of literature could be."

"There is a law in human nature which draws us to be like what we passionately condemn."

"We may fight against what is wrong, but if we allow ourselves to hate, that is to ensure our spiritual defeat and our likeness to what we hate."

These are mere washings in the stream after all the gold in the main seams had been mined. They are chance utterances in the course of some book-review and were never meant to be isolated dicta, but they give the measure of the man's mind.

All my and my wife's labours seemed amply rewarded by the book's success. It was Recommended by the Book Society; it received the cover-page review in *The Times Literary Supplement*, and the *Church Times* gave it a leading article and wrote: "In many ways *The Living Torch* is a better representation of A. E.'s mind and character than any of the books he published in his lifetime." The critic of the *New York Times Book Review* wrote of it:

I am not sure that this is not A. E.'s best book. Having a definite subject and a definite audience in mind kept A. E.'s feet on the ground, prevented him from rising into the vague mysticism which often found vent in weak metaphor and has prejudiced some readers against him. Mr Gibbon's cutting and condensation have, I suspect, strengthened these articles. Reading them one feels that A. E. is talking directly to him, and the personal note of his writing here gives me courage to confess that I have read this book with more excitement than I have read either *The Candle of Vision*, *The National Being* or *The Interpreters*.

Multitudinous reviews poured in from the most unexpected papers, making me feel, more than ever, it was lucky that no shortened forerunner had been allowed to sabotage the volume so far as the critics were concerned.

"If we allow ourselves to hate." Even A. E., who wrote the words, accuses himself of failure to live up to them.

I am a far exile from that great glory which inhabits the

universe, and can but peer through some momentary dusky transparency in my nature to a greater light than the light of day. I know the royal road is by practice of the great virtues. But I cannot speak that language nor urge those obligations, I who have been angry and sensual. I can only speak where I have been faithful. I have never ceased from the inward search, and might by that faithfulness have gone far if I had not a rabble of desires tugging me by the skirts to travel alluring roads in the world of illusion.

Was this one of the passages that irritated Yeats so much when he came to review *Song and its Fountains*? I do not think so. He was a great man, as Lily said, and some part of his being clearly realised that hatred belongs to the more ephemeral side of our nature. It is real, terribly real, but we can escape from it for a moment if we stand back from life and from ourselves. Something of the sort was probably in W. B.'s mind when he wrote for his daughter:

> Considering that, all hatred driven hence,
> The soul recovers radical innocence
> And learns at last that it is self-delighting,
> Self-appeasing, self-affrighting,
> And that its own sweet will is Heaven's will;
> She can, though every face should scowl
> And every windy quarter howl
> Or every bellows burst, be happy still.

A. E., contesting with his rabble of desires, and Yeats, preaching that the soul's sweet will is really Heaven's will, must seem at opposite ends of the dogmatic scale. But in fact they may mean very much the same thing in the end. For it is the *soul's* will that is holy, not the will of the transitory surface self, and it is only when we have driven anger—one of the rabble—out, that we recover innocence.

I cannot pretend to have kept anger out of this book. It is all too evident in its closing pages. But I have tried to be factual and to see things through Yeats's eyes as well as my own. When A. E. came to spend a week-end in

Swanage with Archie Russell in 1934 and heard me telling his host how much I invariably annoyed the poet, he remarked mischievously: "I can't understand how you annoy Yeats so much. You are the only person in Dublin who argues with him and he ought to be grateful to you!" In fact I did not argue a great deal. But if Yeats could read my thoughts—and it is quite possible he could—he must have found me from time to time drawing forbidden comparisons. I did not carp at his achievement like Plato's ghost. I was profoundly impressed by it. But I was continually weighing him in the scales against A. E., and against his own earlier self as expressed in his poems. If I challenged him on something, it was generally the challenge of the over-zealous disciple who thinks certain opinions unfitting to the master. I was too serious. I could not make even a pretence of being worldly and cynical. I expected him to be prophet and teacher as well as poet, and to some extent his habit of summing up a question' in one oracular utterance gave the impression that he assumed this role of prophet, and made it all the more difficult for one to submit to sweeping judgments. For he was not the prophet or the teacher; his generalisations are chaotic, and his judgments, as he himself would have been the first to admit in some calmer moment, were often unsound. In *The Trembling of the Veil* he writes of his fellow-members of the Rhymers' Club: "I think that perhaps our form of lyric, our insistence upon emotion which has no relation to any public interest, gathered together overwrought, unstable men." The insistence upon emotion which has no public interest means that a poet abandons his claim to be anything more than the mouthpiece of a highly personal and subjective viewpoint. There have been poets who did so and were very good poets. But the greatest of all have generally clung to their full prerogative, and have made their poetry a criticism of life. And in fact, from forty onwards, Yeats introduces themes of public interest continually into his

207

verse, but always in a semi-symbolic, slightly chaotic and anarchical fashion. He has none of that overwhelming sense of pity for common humanity which strikes us when we read a writer like Tchekov. He despises the herd and is always harsh in his judgments on it. Conventional morality, conventional religion enrage him, not solely because of their latent insincerity but because they lack the intensity of original sin. The history of mankind is the history of long slow aspiration towards partly-achieved virtues and partly-achieved aims; but such aspirations seem tepid and colourless if weighed in the literary scale, and are colourless when compared either to genuine holiness or to the febrile intensity of unregenerate craving.

Yeats is not a universal poet. He is a subjective poet. When everything is said and done, it comes to this: he retreats into an ivory tower where we are only too glad to follow him. His power over us is based on the fact that he allows us to escape from the disquieting external world into his own disdainful aristocratic world which is so completely different. And to some extent this is the whole *raison d'être* of poets. They are unique individuals, strong enough to reject the banal overtures of the external and to take refuge in themselves. And having mined whatever profundities of thought and feeling lie hidden there, they return and show us the results. Because Yeats has been able to do this, we are grateful to him, and acclaim him. And the further he takes us into his private world the better pleased we are, because of this sense of strangeness and novelty, supreme literary virtues to the jaded appetites of an epoch as late in history as our own. Both Yeats and Joyce are in fact so highly subjective that we can appreciate them properly only after we have made a sufficiently intensive study of their lives. A schoolboy or a navvy can appreciate the greater part of Shakespeare without any gloss, certainly without any biographical elucidation. But Yeats needs to be read in the light of Yeats, and Joyce, so far from being a realist, is a one-man peep-show upon a very limited field of human nature.

Yeats's magic, in his latest work, is achieved by his choice of symbol and by the distinction of his idiom. He may have tried to keep close to the speech—if not to the notions of common men, simply because he realised how great a danger he ran of preciosity; but in fact his speech is always aristocratic and individual. I am inclined to write him down as a pessimist.

> Cast a cold eye
> On life, on death.
> Horseman, pass by!

delighted me, just as it delights everyone, when I first read the words. It seemed the haughty affirmation of our semi-divine nature, the rejection of all the overwhelming pettiness of the world. That was how one should face up to one's mortality, in a spirit of proud detachment. But in fact the words are profoundly pessimistic. He may have intended them to mean that we stand above all ephemeralities. But, even so, it is not our business to cast a cold eye on either life or death. We should look at life with the wondering eye of children and the warm eye of lovers, and in every age where the human spirit has really flowered this has been done. Men had no illusions about life, they were fully aware of its tragic aspects, but they accepted with warmth and gratitude the specific gifts it had to offer. And, similarly, it is not our business to cast a cold eye on death, unless what the poet means is that we should view it with the cold eye of courage. It was Yeats himself who said to me: "Of course death is the great initiator;" and if this is so, to regard it with the cold eye of indifference is scarcely the appropriate advice.

Poets need not be consistent. If they choose to contradict themselves their profession permits it. When Yeats contradicts himself in his poetry, we do not mind. It is merely part of that self-revelation for which we are so grateful. Human nature is contradictory. Our thoughts are not consistent. Many of Yeats's utterances cancel out. On one page we find:

> When a man grows old his joy
> Grows more deep day after day,
> His empty heart is full at length,

and, on another, some fierce attack on age, or the question "Why should not old men be mad?" when they think of the ugly reversals of fortune they have had to witness in the course of their day, such as:

> A girl that knew all Dante once
> Live to bear children to a dunce.

All this is perfectly permissible in a poet whose sensibility, as A. E. said, should be such that it turns to all winds like a weathercock. Yeats raged at life, but he had too much zest for it, and too much delight in the practice of his craft, ever to despair. The one thing that he dreaded was that he should lose his intensity of feeling or his turn of phrase. Sooner than risk that, he preferred to be a foolish passionate man.

His artistry is superb. Even his prose exercises its immediate magic over me, until I come to analyse it. In the last letter which Hone prints we find him writing to Lady Elizabeth Pelham:

In two or three weeks—I am now idle that I may rest after writing much verse—I will begin to write my most fundamental thoughts and the arrangement of thought which I am convinced will complete my studies. I am happy, and I think full of an energy, of an energy I had despaired of. It seems to me that I have found what I wanted. When I try to put all into a phrase I say, "Man can embody truth but he cannot know it." I must embody it in the completion of my life. The abstract is not life and everywhere draws out its contradictions. You can refute Hegel but not the Saint or the Song of Sixpence.

I read the words, and immediately I am amazed and delighted by them. "Man can embody truth but he cannot know it." What discernment, what a sense of standing on the threshold of unrevealed mysteries. I am lost in admiration, but as soon as I begin to reflect on them I realise that they are all false. Of course man cannot know total truth. No sane individual ever imagined he could. But he can know partial truth—and blow himself to pieces with it. He can form concepts and test them in experience. If he is incapable of knowing truth, then for the last four millenniums he has been wasting his time. He should have remained with the antelope and the tiger, who embody it far more effectively than he does. Yeats, when he makes a statement like this—which at first sight so much wins my approval—is really the enemy of philosophy; he becomes the arch-heretic, the apostle of unreason. I know that he meant something, but he did not mean nearly as much as he thought he did. Of course there comes a moment when we must abandon our ratiocinations and rest once more in mere being. But this does not mean that conscious mind was given us merely that we might reject it with contempt. W. B., when he says things like this, is the forerunner of all that body of pseudo-thought which has gradually built itself up into modern sophistry. Though he disliked abstractions, his own dicta have encouraged the cult of wild generalisation.

I am arguing with him once more. Some basic antithesis always declares itself when I come up against his thought. I say to myself, "This man is not interested in truth.* He is interested only in vivid, colourful and compelling half-truths, and because he is such a superb poet he makes these half-truths glow with inner light." But that does not absolve him from his philosophic responsibilities. He is the angry old man, forerunner of all the angry young men who

* Cp. the phrase in his letter to Robert Graves: "Too reasonable, too truthful. We poets should be good liars."

are shortly to come. Even in literature his influence has
been in some degree detrimental. Because his use of symbolic idiom was so effective, a whole generation presently
grew up who imagined that poetry could discard not only
logic but all formal thought, and subsist like a rootless
plant on a jumble of exotic images and curious adjacencies.
Apollo requires more than that of his votaries. One must
never forget that he is also the god of light.

XXIV

YEATS died on the Riviera on 28 January 1939. I must have written to Lily expressing my sympathy to his sisters and my homage to the poet, and presumably maintaining a tactful silence where our personal contacts were concerned, for I find her writing to me on 22 April 1939:

My dear Willy Monk

Yes—we did get your letter of sympathy and were very grateful to you. I did not write then as I had so many letters to answer—over 200 and also sent cards to people I only knew a little.

I quite saw that Willy's life would not be for much longer, but I hoped for another year or two—he and I were such close friends all our lives—he exhilarated me I felt full of life and light after being with him. We never had a tiff since we banged each other in the nursery.

He was so vivid and vital—his house even now feels full of him—and he kept his good looks to the end—there was no going to pieces which he would have so much disliked—Dermot O'Brien says that as he lay dead he looked beautiful, he says he always thought him handsome, but till then he had not realised how very handsome he was.

He wrote a poem and finished a play a day or so before—and was extremely happy.

His end was peaceful—an attack of pain and breathlessness came at 5 a.m.—the doctors came and gave morphia—his very rapid breathing became slower and ceased about 2 p.m. and he had gone.

He is to lie finally in Drumcliff—probably in September. The spot has been chosen by Mrs W. B. and Jack—as he wished, at the foot of Ben Bulben.

Our great grandfather Rev. John Yeats was rector there from

1811 to 1846—then a big parish supporting two curates and the rector's racehorses.

Write again and I hope I have not only confused your family history.

We come of good stock—they lived strenuous lives with courage and strength and brains.

Ten years before, in some discussion about the problem of the minority in Ireland, she had written very much the same sentiments to me:

We must stand up for ourselves again but do it with Art—not just sugar and honey poured out with shut eyes—we are of good stock and have lived hard lives with cheerful hearts, and all I think are full of the hope of heaven which is a fine backbone to us.

She was no older in spirit now than when I had first known her and had walked beside her as a schoolboy down Abbey Street on our way to the theatre. Later in 1939 I quoted, in an article I had written, a remark which she had once made to me apropos of our yearly migration from Donegal to Dorset: "You are right to come back each year. Every child should have a paradise; our paradise as children was Sligo."

7 May 1939

My dear Willy Monk

Many thanks for the paper. I like your article and feel proud to be quoted.

It was not just a thought that passed through my mind but a firm belief. We had our paradise as children and it has never left us—or perhaps I ought to say we have never left it—no-one will ever see Sligo again as we saw it.

Willy had kept his paradise—his wish to leave his body there showed that.

I saw your name among the list of subscribers to the Hall at Drumcliff. G. B. S. and his wife sent £50—which ought to cheer the heart of the Rector.

J. M. Hone has started on the life and has been over to see me several times—he sighs and makes notes and sighs again—

but is I think quite happy and enjoying the work—he expects to be about two years over it.

There is an enormous amount of material to be gone through . . .

Your mother and Mary took me for a lovely drive the other day—we went to Bray and handed newly-mended shoes over a gate to John [my schoolboy nephew] who was playing cricket on a field so green it looked as if it was not real.

Then we went on and handed a parcel over a hedge to Valerie [a niece] who clad in bright pink was playing tennis with other pink maidens in a shady place as green as the field John was in.

I did enjoy the drive—your Mother and Mary are both quick-minded—I find people you have to say even very unimportant things several times over before they take it in very exhausting —but they take up one's note at once.

We have had a lovely spell of hot weather—clear, serene weather—very lovely.

I open the door as I go up to bed and sniff the night—full of sweet smell—the lilac is going over but the may is out and there is no darkness—only a half-dark.

Donegal must be beautiful.

I can only find three more letters of hers after this. One is enquiring about some common ancestor "Anne, daughter of Meredith Lloyd, who in 1723 married Abraham Butler." Another, dated 19 Sept 1939, runs:

My dear Willy Monk

Well, that was a very pleasant talk we had, thank you very much for ringing me up.

Here is the photograph [taken by Fred MacCormick of W. B. seated on a sofa in the window of Lennox Robinson's house in Killiney]. I think it is very good—the lift or turn of his head gives him a too small chin, that is all.

I am always glad that he kept his good looks to the end.

We are going to pieces—he went with his flag flying.

I miss him all the time—his going has left a great loneliness behind with me.

I hope things for all may be better soon

Yours affectionately
Lily Yeats.

Her last letter is dated 2 February 1940. Lolly had died and she writes:

My dear Willy Monk

Thank you so much for your kind sympathy. Lolly did not suffer much and went out quickly and is I am sure as vivid and active now as she was in this life—I believe with Willy when he said "behind all this is reality."

She is buried here at Churchtown. The Rector and the Dean of St Patrick's held the service—and I am glad the great chapter from Corinthians was read—it is like a magnificent orchestra of certainty.

I have heard your father read it as one of the lessons, while not even the most featherheaded in the congregation moved, they seemed hardly to breathe. He had a fine sense of the beauty of words.

Lolly and I have had a most strenuous life—clogged always by want of money. We kept the industry going through the war, the rebellion, the civil war—postal strikes in which I had stolen £28 of embroidery—railway strikes—general strikes—in the civil war we were raided and three of our workers carried off—they came back six weeks later and we never asked what had happened and they said not a word—the cottage was surrounded—a man with a revolver at each window and door. I was alone with the girls at the time, they went on as if nothing was happening, some ironing, others printing, others damping papers, others at embroidery.

As soon as the men had gone in their Crossley lorries one girl exclaimed, "Thank God Miss Lolly was not here."

Lolly came soon after. I went to meet her and told her.

"Well, I wasn't here," she said. "I would have been sure to bite someone."

I think few know that Lolly was the inventor of "brushwork" and published four books on it when in her twenties and drew a nice income from royalties for years. It revolutionised the art teaching in schools.

Lolly left her Cuala set of books and all her first editions of Irish authors to Trinity Hall to found a library to be called "The Elizabeth Yeats Library." Your books are among them. Miss Cunningham is very pleased and it is to be kept under lock and key—in special bookshelves—there are almost 300 books in all.

I am pleased to think we sitting under the gallery made you feel in touch with literature [I had told her evidently what I have told the reader at the beginning of this book]. I don't think we ever felt ourselves in any way interesting or apart—life was such hard work we had no time for pride.

Jack and I can't endure noise or fuss of any sort. Jack always gets his own way all the same—my line is passive resistance.

I am now alone in the house once so full of laughter and good talk. Your mother was kind enough to come and see me last week, in fact she came twice but the first time I could not see her, as the doctor had given me dope and sent me to bed for three days. I slept most of the time and felt the better for it.

I am sorry to hear your Uncle George is dead.

Love to Winifred, all is well I hope, and to you,

From
Your affectionate cousin
Lily Yeats.

I had a good letter from Masefield.
The Press is to go on.   L. Y.

She herself was to follow Lolly in five years' time. She was still alive when T. S. Eliot flew to Dublin in 1942 to deliver the first Yeats Memorial Lecture at the Abbey Theatre. I happened to be down from Donegal, where I was then living, and I went to the lecture with my nephew. There a strange fate befell me. I was standing in the foyer about ten minutes before the lecture was due to begin when Sean O'Faolain came up to me in some perturbation.

"You must propose the vote of thanks to Eliot."

"Oh no, I can't."

"You must. You've written lots about Yeats. You know it all."

"I have never published a line about Yeats in my life."

"Well, you know what to say."

"Why this last-minute search for a speaker?"

"Well, the man who was to have done it won't."

"I'll do it on one condition, that I don't have to come

down to the stage but can speak from my place in the balcony."

"All right. Anything you like."

I went up to the circle. I had ten minutes in which to think of what I had to say and jot down a few headings on the back of an envelope. There were Mrs W. B., Anne and Michael sitting immediately in front of me. I had better break it to them. It might be a shock for Mrs W. B. if I rose suddenly in my seat. I leaned over and whispered to Mrs Yeats, "O'Faolain is making me propose the vote of thanks."

Eliot delivered his lecture. His tone was subdued and I had to wait until I read it later in the pages of the *Kenyon Review* to realise its full merit. Now it was over. I was for it. I rose to my feet. I told them I was the ram caught in the thicket at the last minute. I did not know who Isaac was [I learnt later that he was Hone, sitting below me in the stalls] but whoever he was I had been dragged from my thicket to save him from sacrifice. Literature liked the gallant gesture, such as the gesture of his fellow-scribes who threw their manuscripts into Spenser's grave, or the gesture, on the present occasion, of a great English poet flying the Irish Channel in wartime in order to speak to us in praise of a great Irish poet. We could do with such gestures. The individual of genius was rare, but the family of genius was rarer still. I instanced the Rossetti family, and I instanced, now, the four children of John Butler Yeats and named them in turn.

And then—for one must not be a humbug, even in the Abbey Theatre and before a packed house—I told them that I had never been in Yeats's company for five minutes without infuriating him. But that was beside the point. He was a great poet, and every younger writer in the country stood deeply in his debt, because he had turned the eyes of the world upon Ireland. Mr Eliot had dealt chiefly with the later poetry. I was still loyal to the earlier. And suddenly I had launched forth on it and was chanting to them, over the head of the seated Mrs Yeats, the swinging rhythm and melody of

All things uncomely and broken, all things worn out and old,
The cry of a child by the roadway, the creak of a lumbering cart,
The heavy steps of the ploughman, splashing the wintry mould,
Are wronging your image that blossoms a rose in the deeps of my
 heart.

I chanted that to them; I chanted some of the earlier love poetry. He had omitted it all from his anthology, but it was going to come into its own again, for a minute or two, now. It had bound me with a spell years before, and it did so once again, as I drew it from memory for these strangers.

XXV

SOMETIMES I think that my quarrels with Yeats were really Yeats's own quarrel with himself. His personality was riven by an internal discord. I wanted to think of him as a young tree ablaze with blossom, whereas, when we met, he was a gnarled oak cleft and blackened by lightning. He could feel this and he resented it. A. E. seemed all of a piece. I suspect that if I had met A. E. in early manhood I should have thought him something of a crank and a faddist. Many of his utterances are highly rhetorical and a little absurd. Nevertheless his general direction never changed. The perfervid A. E. of youth became the balanced, serene, bearded A. E. that we all loved. As he matured, his nature veered away, not from *Patanjali* or the *Bhagavad-gita*, but from the pseudo-mystical extravagances of some of the theosophical friends with whom he had first entered on the path. His mind tended to align itself more with Plato and the Greeks. He might complain that as he aged the walls of the psyche thickened, and that he felt "a far wanderer from that great glory." But in fact he never became a stranger to himself, whereas Yeats did. A. E. could write:

I know, when I come to my own immortal, I will find there
In a myriad instant all that the wandering soul found fair.

Yeats gave the impression of having turned his back on his own immortal, so that even to remind him of it was an offence.

I am not alone in thinking this. I have Maud Gonne's support for it. I have Yeats's own. "I choose the second-best." The very fact that my own bias of temperament lay a good deal nearer to Yeats's made me all the harsher critic of him. I had none of A. E.'s heroic tenacity and calm. I had all Yeats's impatience, and some at least of his pugnacity. It came naturally therefore to me to hero-worship A. E. and to condemn Yeats.

W. B. must have been dead seven or eight years when I found myself one day in bed, laid low with a cold, and reading T. R. Henn's excellent book, *The Lonely Tower*. Its opening chapters brought back all my early impressions of the poems. I saw Yeats in terms of his youth and Sligo days, and then I passed on to encounter the different phases as seen through this shrewd critic's eyes. Presently a couple of lines shaped themselves in my mind suddenly, expressing completely my own personal impression of the W. B. I had known:

> That wrong-headed old man,
> Whose phrase was always right.

One may have no idea whatever, on an occasion like this, what direction a poem is going to take. I had none now. But if one feels a poem in the air, one has only to wait and, presently, if the intimation is right and the Muse is favourable, something will come. What came was a strange mingling and blending; a quotation from *Hamlet*, a recollection of the three triumvirs pricking off names in the tent before Philippi, a recollection of Yeats's own assertion that without anger and lust his later-day Muse would be completely silenced: and, finally, the thought that it was only when Roman religion was already almost dead that men exalted the gold image of Augustus to a place in the temple, as a substitute for their once seriously-held spiritual convictions. In somewhat the same way, when purpose dies in literature, men tend to exalt verbal felicity.

I wrote:

ON RE-READING YEATS

That wrong-headed old man,
Whose phrase was always right,

221

Casts his potent spell
Across the mind tonight.
"Words, words, words!"
But the words are always right.

Within his tented soul
Anger and pride and lust
Prick off the hated names,
Proscribing, as they must—
Haughty triumvirate—
The patient humble dust.

Plato is mocked, the mob
Receives its scornful due.
Destiny, death itself,
Is fashioned anew
In a gold phrase which may—
Perhaps—be true.

When Caesar, having torn
The world asunder, set
An image of perfect gold
Above the fever and fret,
In the stilled temples men
Accepted it.

THE END

INDEX